The Compact Book of

Crochet Stitches

First published in 2021 by Sona Books
an imprint of Danann Media Publishing Ltd.

CAT NO: SON0543
ISBN: 978-1-915343-81-9
Made in the UAE.

Welcome to
The Compact Book of
Crochet Stitches

Crochet has boomed in recent years, offering craft lovers a new way to make thoughtful gifts, inexpensive accessories and homemade decorations. *The Compact Book of Crochet Stitches* is the perfect companion for crochet crafters of any skill level that are looking to discover fun and creative new stitches. Packed with all of the basic techniques to refresh your memory, this book contains all of the information that you need to complete an array of stitches that will mean you can tackle your next crochet project with confidence.

Contents

The Essentials

Going Further

Edges & Finishes

Reference

45

Contents

The Essentials

Get started and learn the basics that will lay the foundations of all of your crochet projects.

"A crochet hook can feel a bit unnatural in your hand at first, but you'll soon get used to the way it feels"

Reading charted stitch diagrams

Some crocheters find these visual representations of crochet patterns easier to follow than a written-out pattern

Made up of symbols to represent stitches, charted stitch diagrams lay out a pattern in a visual way, and will look similar to the actual piece of crocheted fabric. The symbols are uniform and internationally recognised, so you will be able to follow them with ease.

Diagrams (sometimes also called charts) can often be found accompanying written-out patterns but may also sometimes be used instead of them, especially for particularly detailed patterns such as lace work and motifs. To begin with it may be best to read a chart alongside a written pattern. Even if using a diagram becomes your preferred method of following a pattern, don't completely disregard written instructions, as these will include important information about special stitches and any repeats you may need to make.

Standard stitch symbols

The symbols for the most commonly used stitches and techniques are designed to look like the stitches they represent. The treble crochet symbol is twice as tall as the double crochet symbol, with the half treble crochet halfway between the two. The horizontal bars on the taller stitches represent how many yarn overs need to be made to begin the stitch. Use the table below to see what stitches the symbols represent:

Symbol	Stitch
	ch
 or 	sl st
 or 	dc
	htr
	tr
	dtr
	magic ring

Variable stitch symbols

When the basic stitches are combined to make special stitches — such as puffs, popcorns, bobbles and shells to name just a few — the stitch diagram represents this, showing the exact combination of basic stitches that is used in the pattern you are following. These may be different from pattern to pattern if the stitches are made in slightly different ways. Here are a few examples of special stitches:

Symbol	Stitch
	dc2tog decrease
	tr3tog cluster/decrease
	5-dtr shell
	4-tr bobble
	3-htr puff
	4-tr popcorn
	ch-3 picot (closed)
	ch-3 picot (open)

"Symbols of crochet charts have been designed to look like the stitches they represent"

Modified stitch symbols

When you need to work the next stitch into a specific part of a stitch — for example in the back or front loop only or around the back or front of the post stitch below — the stitch symbol is modified to represent this. Stitches that need to be worked into the front or back loop only include a curved symbol below them to represent this. Stitches that need to be worked around the front or back post are shown with a hook on the bottom. Foundation stitches show the stitch joined to the chain below. When stitches are crossed, the stitch that needs to go behind the other is slightly more faded than the one that sits to the front:

Symbol	Stitch
	FPtr
	BPtr
	dc in back loop only
	dc in front loop only
	foundation dc
	crossed trs

How to read a chart

Now that you have our handy reference tables to determine what all the different crochet symbols mean, you will need to know how to put them together in an actual piece of crochet. The diagram below represents the stitches as you will see them from the right side of the work (as opposed to the wrong side), and you will notice that each stitch is shown above the one that it needs to be crocheted into.

When working in rows from a stitch diagram, you almost always begin with the foundation chain and then start to work Row 1 from right to left. When you get to Row 2 if you are turning your work, you need to work from left to right. All subsequent odd rows should be followed from right to left and even rows from left to right.

When working in rounds (for example when crocheting granny squares), start from the central ring and follow the stitches in a counterclockwise direction. Do this for every round, unless an arrow at the start of the round indicates to change direction. In this case, turn the work and follow the pattern around clockwise.

> "When working in rounds (for example when crocheting granny squares), start from the central ring and follow stitches in a counterclockwise direction"

TOP TIP

Even rows are normally shown in a different colour than the odd rows, as this helps distinguish which stitches belong to which row.

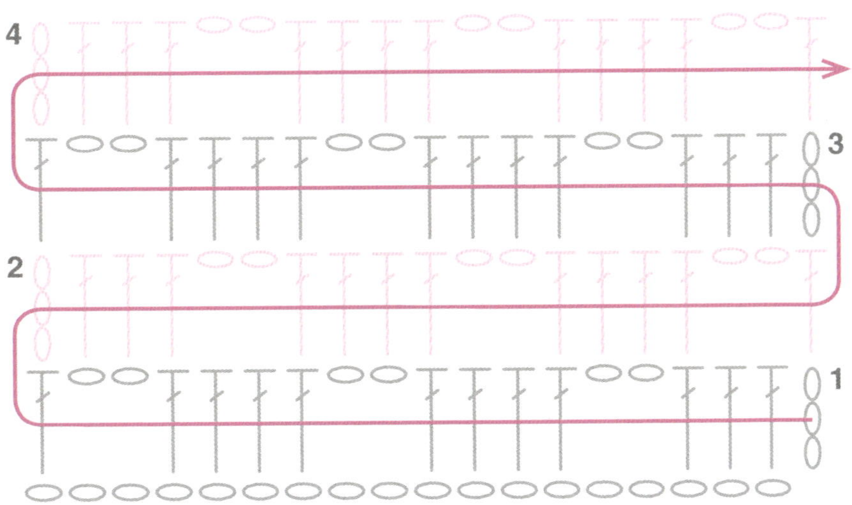

Making a foundation chain

When working in rows to make a piece of flat crocheted fabric, you will need to create a foundation chain to work your first row of stitches into

A solid foundation

Make your base

01 Start with a slipknot

The first step is to create a slipknot on your hook.

02 Yarn over

Move your hook underneath your yarn to create a yarn over.

03 Pull through

Move the hook back through the loop already on your hook, making sure to catch the working yarn. You have now made your first chain.

04 Keep going

Repeat Steps 02 and 03 to make more chains. Hold the stitches you've already made in your left hand close to the hook for stability. Your pattern will tell you how many you need to chain.

Making stitches

01 Even stitches

Try to make all the chains a similar size to ensure you are making a strong foundation for your piece. If some are very loose and others aren't, the effect will be a wavy edge to your piece. This will take some practice.

02 Not too tight

It's best to keep the chains quite loose to begin with, as tight chains will be very difficult to make stitches in when it comes to the next row, as you will struggle to insert your hook into them and pull it through again.

Counting chains

When beginning a project, the pattern you are following will tell you how many chains you need to create, either in total or as a multiple. It's important to create exactly the right number, as getting this wrong will mean you have to unravel your work when you find out you've either got too many or not enough at the end of your first row. To count the chains, identify the Vs on the side that's facing you. Each of these is one chain. The V above the slipknot is your first chain, but do not count the loop on your hook. This is the working loop and does not count as a chain. If you are creating a very long chain, it might help to mark every ten or 20 stitches with a stitch marker.

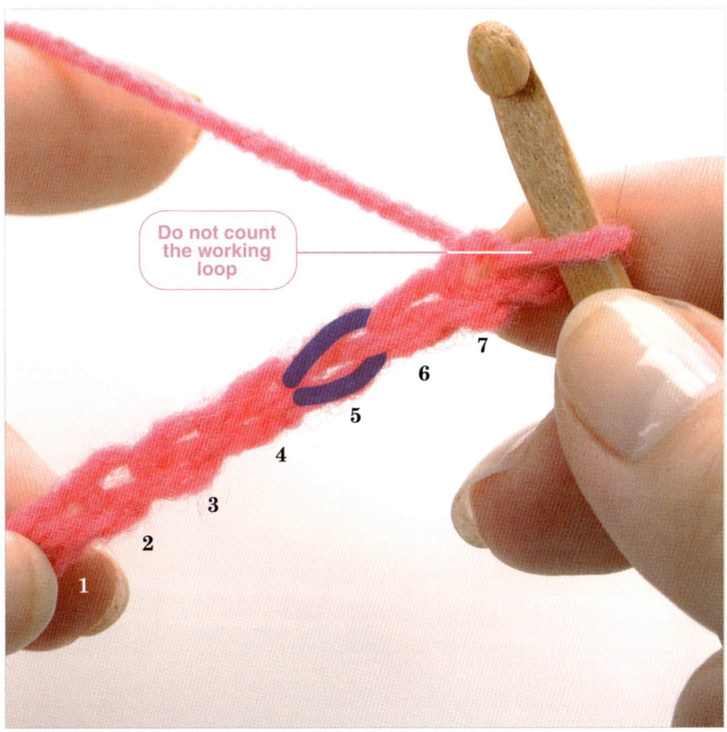

Did you know?

When you become more confident, you could try the more advanced foundation double crochet, which creates a foundation chain and the first row of double crochet stitches at the same time. For more information, see page 18.

Working the chain

Now you've made your foundation chain, it's time to get going on your project by creating your first row of stitches into the chain

Get to know the foundation chain

01 Front of the chain

Looking at the front side of your chain, you will see a row of sideways Vs, each with a top loop and a bottom loop.

02 Back of the chain

When you look at the back side of the chain, you will see a line of bumps in between the loops. These are called the back bumps.

Under the top loop

01 Find the top loop

For this method, hook under the top loop only.

02 Insert your hook

Move your hook to insert it under the top loop of a V.

Under the top loop and back bump

01 Under two
Hooking under both the top loop and the back bump is sometimes referred to as the top two loops of the chain.

02 Insert your hook
Move your hook to insert it under the back bump and top loop of a chain.

Under the back bump

01 Find the back bump
Turn over your chain so that the back bumps are facing you.

02 Insert your hook
Move your hook to insert it under the back bump.

Be consistent
It doesn't matter which method you use as long as you are consistent when moving along the chain. Working under the top loop is the easiest method for beginners, but does not create as neat an edge as working under the back bumps. With practice you'll find the most comfortable method for you.

Chainless foundations

If you've got to grips with chains, why not try creating your first row without making any chains first?

Creating your foundation chain and the subsequent first row of crochet can sometimes result in the chain becoming twisted, but this can be avoided by starting your project with a chainless foundation instead. This combines the foundation chain and the first row in one initial row of crochet rather than two. Using a chainless foundation is a great way to create a stretchy edging compared to a more rigid chain start. Given that you are working the two rows at once, it does take a little longer to work up the chainless foundation than a foundation chain, but it is easier to work your second row into the chainless foundation than into the chain, as you don't have to worry about your chain becoming too tight or twisting while you work into it.

Foundation double crochet (fdc)

Create your first two rows at once

01 Chain two

To get going, the first step in creating your foundation double crochet (fdc) is to chain two. You will be making your first crochet into the second chain from the hook.

02 Insert your hook

Insert your hook into the second chain your from hook, yarn over (yo) and draw up a loop.

Strong foundation

Chainless foundation stitches form vertically so the chain part of the stitch is at the bottom, on the left, and the tops of the stitches are formed on the right.

03 Create the chain

Now yarn over once more and pull the yarn through the first loop on your hook. This forms the chain stitch that you will create your first double crochet (dc) into.

04 Yarn over

Now yarn over your hook and pull through the two loops that are on your hook. You have now created your first double crochet.

05 Keep going

Each following foundation double crochet is worked into the two loops that form the chain at the bottom of the stitch you have just worked.

06 Create your next double crochet

Insert your hook under the top and back loops of the chain, yarn over and draw up the loop. Make sure it is level before you continue to work the stitch. If you make it too tight it will be difficult to start your next stitch. Now repeat Steps 03 and 04, repeating until you've made the right number of stitches.

Create longer chainless foundation stitches

You don't just have to create your first row with double crochets; you can create longer stitches simply by following the same system. You can create a chainless foundation with half treble (htr) and treble (tr) crochets. You merely have to complete the stitch in the same way as you usually would once you have created the 'chain' that you will be working into.

Double crochet

Master the basics by learning the simplest stitch

Double crochet (dc) is a very important stitch in crochet as it is one of the simplest, and therefore the one that most crocheters tend to learn to use first. Mastering this stitch will also help you when it comes to creating taller stitches, as most are created by just adding steps to the method for making a double crochet.

Using only double crochets creates a very compact, dense fabric, which makes it great for thick, warm winter garments. It is also a very common stitch in amigurumi and toy making, as the compact fabric created is very good for holding stuffing in. You will be able to create a variety of projects just by mastering this stitch.

If you plan to double crochet into a foundation chain, as we will in this tutorial, then you will need to make one more chain than the number of stitches you want to create, as the first stitch is never worked into the first chain from the hook. However, this will be accounted for in a pattern, so always chain the number stated.

A solid foundation

Make your base

01 Foundation chain

Make a foundation chain to the required length. If you just want to practise, start by making about 20 chains. If you want to make a piece exactly 20 stitches wide, chain 21.

02 Insert hook

Identify the second chain from your hook and then insert your hook here.

03 Draw up a loop

Yarn over (yo), then draw up a loop. You will now have two loops on your crochet hook.

04 Pull through two

Yarn over and then draw the yarn through both loops on the hook so you have one loop left on your hook. You have completed the stitch.

05 Keep going

Continue making double crochets by inserting your hook into each remaining chain and repeating Steps 03 and 04. When you have finished the row, chain one.

06 Time to turn

Turn your work counterclockwise, so that the next stitches ready to be worked into are to the left of the hook.

07 Start a new row

Identify the first stitch of the row (not the turning chain). Insert your hook here.

08 Repeat

Follow Step 03 and 04 to complete the stitch.

Keep counting

Remember to count your stitches as you go along, especially when you're learning. It's easy to add in an extra stitch at the beginning or miss one off the end, and counting how many you have will alert you to a mistake at the earliest opportunity.

Treble crochet

This stitch is twice the size of the single crochet, and worked in a very similar way

The treble crochet (tr) is a very common stitch that is simple to create, especially once you've mastered the technique of making a double crochet (dc). It is created simply by adding a couple of steps to the method for creating a double crochet.

Due to its increased height, this stitch creates a much less compact and therefore more versatile fabric than the double crochet. It is a very common and recognisable stitch, as seen in granny squares. When working a treble crochet into a foundation chain, you must make two more chains than your desired number of stitches. This is because a treble crochet is usually worked into the fourth chain from the hook when being worked into a foundation chain, and the three unworked chains will form your first treble crochet stitch.

Building up your skill

Make a treble crochet

01 Foundation chain

Make a foundation chain to the required length. For a precise number of stitches, chain that many plus two. Find the fourth chain from the hook.

02 Yarn over

Make a yarn over (yo) and then insert your hook into the fourth chain from the hook.

03 Draw up a loop

Yarn over, then draw up a loop. There should now be three loops on your hook.

04 Pull through two

Yarn over, then draw the yarn through two of the loops on your hook. There should now be two loops on your hook.

05 Complete the stitch

Yarn over and then draw the yarn through the two loops left on the hook. You have completed the stitch and should now have one loop on your hook.

06 Keep going

Continue making treble crochets by making a yarn over and then inserting your hook into each remaining chain and repeating Steps 3 to 5. When you have finished the row, chain three.

07 Turn

Turn your work counterclockwise ready to start the next row. The two chains you just made count as the first stitch, so your next stitch will need to be made in the second stitch of the row.

08 Continue down the row

Yarn over, put your hook into the next stitch and repeat Steps 3 to 5 to make the stitch. Continue to the end of the row, remembering to put the final treble into the top of the turning chain of the row below.

> "This stitch creates a much less compact and therefore more versatile fabric than the double crochet"

Half treble crochet

It's less common and sits between double and treble crochet in height, but the half treble is still important

This stitch is strange when compared to the double crochet (dc) and treble crochet (tr) in the way that it's made. Instead of drawing a loop through two loops, the yarn is instead pulled through three to create a half treble crochet (htr). This produces a stitch that's about half as tall as the treble crochet, but taller than the double crochet. This can be quite tricky to get the hang of the first time, so a little practice may be necessary. When used on its own, the half treble crochet produces a fairly compact fabric, which is similar in texture to that created when using double crochet by itself. Mastering the techniques used to create the double and treble crochet will help greatly when creating the half treble crochet.

Like with working a double crochet into a foundation chain, you will need to make one more chain than your desired number of stitches. This is because the treble crochet will be worked into the third chain from the hook, and the two unworked chains will form your first half treble crochet stitch.

Combining techniques

Make a half treble crochet

01 Foundation chain
Make a foundation chain to the required length, not forgetting to chain one more than the number of stitches you desire. Identify the third chain from the hook.

02 Yarn over
Make a yarn over (yo), and then insert your hook into the third chain from the hook.

03 Draw up a loop
Yarn over, then draw up a loop. There should now be three loops on your hook.

04 Pull through three
Yarn over, then draw the yarn through all three loops on your hook. The stitch is now complete and there should be one loop on your hook.

05 Keep going

Continue making half treble crochets by making a yarn over, inserting your hook into each remaining chain and repeating Steps 03 and 04. When you have finished the row, chain two.

06 Turn

Turn your work counterclockwise ready to start the next row. The two chains you just made count as the first stitch, so your next stitch will need to be made in the second stitch of the row.

07 Start new row

Yarn over and insert your hook into the second stitch of the row.

08 Continue to crochet

Repeat Steps 03 and 04 to complete the stitch.

Double treble crochet

This common stitch is much taller than the treble crochet, and this size allows it to be worked into a piece of fabric fairly quickly

While the other stitches you have learned create quite close, compact stitches, the double treble crochet (dtr) creates very tall stitches that make a loose, stretchy fabric. For this reason, the double treble crochet is most often found in lace work.

The double treble crochet is created by making two yarn overs (yo) before inserting the hook into the stitch or chain below, and this can make it quite fiddly to work with. It's important to check that you have the correct number of loops on your hook after you've drawn up the first loop, as it's very easy for the second yarn over to slip off the hook before you insert it into your fabric, without you even noticing. However, this is a valuable stitch because when compared to the double crochet (dc), which works up rather slowly, it's very easy to create a large piece of fabric quickly with the double treble crochet.

When creating a foundation chain to work double treble crochets into, you need to make three more chains than the desired number of stitches, as the first stitch will be worked into the fifth chain from the hook, with the four chains making the first double treble crochet stitch.

The tallest stitch

Make the double treble crochet

01 Foundation chain

Make a foundation chain to the required length, making sure to chain three more than the number of stitches you need. Identify the fifth chain from the hook.

02 Yarn over twice

Make two yarn overs and then insert your hook into the fifth chain from the hook.

03 Draw up a loop

Yarn over and draw up a loop. There should be four loops on your hook.

04 Pull through two

Yarn over, then draw the yarn through two of the loops on your hook. There should now be three loops on your hook.

05 And again...

Yarn over, then draw the yarn through two of the loops on your hook again. There should now be two loops on your hook.

06 ...and once more

Yarn over, then draw the yarn through the two loops on your hook. There should now be one loop on your hook.

07 Complete the row

Repeat Steps 02 to 06 into each remaining chain to finish the row. When you reach the end of the row, chain four and turn your work clockwise. The chain four counts as the first stitch, so you will need to make the next into the second stitch from the end.

08 Carry on crocheting

Yarn over twice, insert the hook into the second stitch from the end of the row and repeat Steps 03 to 06 to complete the stitch.

Slip stitch

While rarely used on its own to create a pattern, this versatile stitch is really handy for joining stitches and moving the position of the hook and yarn without adding height

Function over style

Make the slip stitch (sl st)

01 Foundation chain

Make a foundation chain to the required length. For a precise number of stitches, chain that many plus one. Identify the second chain from your hook.

02 Into chain

Insert your hook into the second chain from the hook. Yarn over (yo).

03 Draw up a loop

Pull your hook back through the chain. There should be two loops on your hook.

04 Pull through

Avoiding the urge to yarn over, continue to pull the yarn through the second loop on the hook. You have completed the stitch and should have one loop on your hook. Repeat Steps 02 to 04 to finish the row.

05 Turn clockwise

There will be very few instances in which you need to crochet more than one row of slip stitches. However, if you do, begin by turning the yarn clockwise when you reach the end of the row, so the working yarn is towards the back.

06 Which stitch?

There's no turning chain with a slip stitch, so you will need to make your first stitch into the first stitch of the row.

07 Front or back

Your pattern should specify whether to make your next stitch in the front or back loop of the stitch, as slip stitch is rarely worked under both loops. Insert your hook under the loop specified in your pattern.

08 Continue

Repeat Steps 03 and 04 to make the slip stitch.

> "There will be very few instances in which you need to crochet more than one row of slip stitches"

Identifying and counting stitches

All crocheted fabric is made up of different kinds of stitches, but learning what those stitches look like on their own is essential to creating your own work

With the guides in this book you will already have discovered how to create a foundation chain, as well as different kinds of stitches like double crochet (dc), treble crochet (tr) and half treble crochet (htr). While it is important to know how to create these stitches, it is also necessary to know what those stitches look like in your work so that you know how to count and build upon them. It can be daunting at first to look at what you've crocheted and to try to count the stitches you have just made, however if you follow these simple steps you'll see just what your fabric is made of.

Identifying stitches

Each stitch is made up of a post (which differs in height depending on the stitch worked) and a V (which consists of a front loop and a back loop). The V sits slightly to the right of the post.

The Vs are the stitches most commonly worked into. If you turn your work at the end of a row, the Vs that you work into will be pointing to the left. Insert your hook underneath the V that is slightly to the left of the post.

If you do not turn your work at the end of each row (for example if you're working in the round), then the Vs that you will be working into will point to the right. In this instance, insert your hook underneath the V that is sat slightly to the right of the post.

Counting chains

There are two ways to count stitches: either by counting the Vs along the top of the work or by counting the posts. If you count the Vs, make sure you never count the loop that is on your hook. When counting either Vs or posts, you must take careful consideration when you come to the turning chain. If it is counted as a stitch in your pattern, then count it, but if not, leave it out.

Counting rows

Counting the posts is the easiest way to count how many rows you've crocheted. When working with tall stitches, such as those made by a treble crochet, these will be easy to identify and count no matter how you're working with them. However, when working with shorter stitches, such as those made by a double crochet, the stitches can look different depending on whether you're turning your work or not.

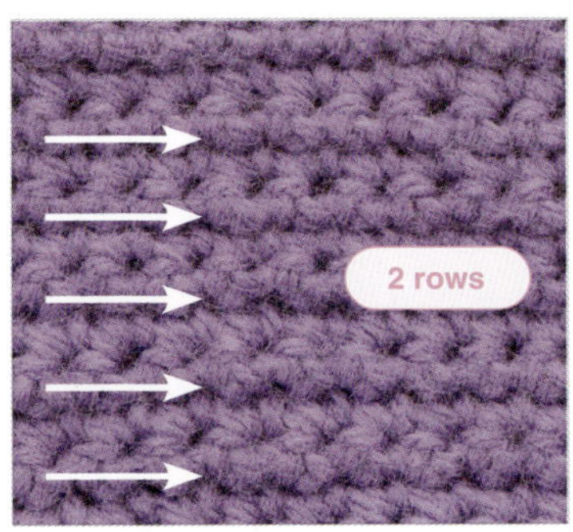

When using double crochet in rows and turning your work, what looks like one distinct post is actually made up of two rows, as you're seeing the front and the back of the stitch. This makes it easier to count them in twos.

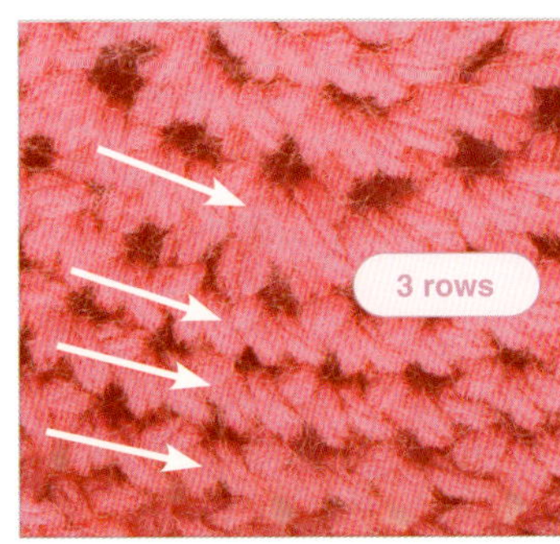

When using double crochet and working in the round, the stitches are more distinct as you're only seeing the front of the stitch in every round. This makes them much easier to count in single rounds.

"Counting the posts is the easiest way to count how many rows you've crocheted"

Increasing

To increase the number of stitches in a row, simply crochet two or more into the same stitch

Increasing is a very useful technique in crochet and one that's incredibly easy to execute. Increasing is essential when working in the round to create something flat, as the extra stitches add width. Without increasing, you would just build upwards, not outwards. Increasing is also very useful when shaping items — such as amigurumi — as it can be combined with decreases to make the shapes you need.

To increase the number of stitches in your round or row, simply crochet two or more stitches into one stitch of the row below.

For example, if you have just crocheted a round of eight stitches, then crochet two of each stitch into each stitch below — your next round will have 16 stitches. In patterns, increasing is written as the number of stitches to be made into the stitch below. For example, '2 tr in next st'.

TOP TIP

Making lots of increases in one place will make bulges (and shells), so if you just want to make the piece larger without distorting the fabric, spread your increases out across the length of the round or row.

Adding stitches

Make a treble crochet increase in the next stitch (2 tr in next st)

01 Treble crochet

Make a treble crochet in the next stitch.

02 Into the same stitch

Make another treble crochet in the same stitch. You have increased your stitch count by one.

Increasing at the start of a row

Make a treble crochet increase in the next stitch (2 tr in next st)

01 Chain three and turn

As the turning chain normally counts as a stitch (except in double crochet), increasing at the start of a row is slightly different.

02 Into the first stitch

Where you would normally make your first stitch into the second stitch from the hook, to increase, insert your hook into the first stitch at the base of the chain and make the stitch.

03 Two stitches

The stitch you've just made and the turning chain count as two stitches, and you have made an increase.

Decreasing

Often worked in conjunction with increases when shaping crochet, decrease stitches reduce the number of stitches in a row

While the easiest way to reduce the number of stitches in a row is to simply skip stitches, this creates a hole, which is not always the desired effect. To avoid this hole, decrease stitches work multiple stitches together, thereby eliminating stitches while also filling in the gap. Decrease stitches are named after the number and type of stitches being crocheted together. For example, 'dc2tog' means that two double crochet stitches will be combined into one. When the number in the middle increases, this means even more stitches will be crocheted into one. While decreases have many different names and forms, the basic formula is the same: make all the stitches up to the final step so that they are all on the hook, then complete all the stitches together.

Double crochet two stitches together (dc2tog)

Combine two double crochet stitches

01 Insert hook

Insert your hook into the next stitch, as if to make a double crochet. Draw up a loop.

02 Insert hook again

Without completing the stitch, insert your hook into the next stitch as if to make another double crochet. Draw up a loop. You should now have three loops on your hook.

03 Through three

Yarn over (yo) and draw the loop through all three stitches on your hook. Having worked into two stitches, but only created one, you have decreased by one.

Treble crochet three stitches together (tr3tog)

Combine three stitches

01 Insert hook

Yarn over and insert your hook into the next stitch, as if to make a treble crochet. Draw up a loop, yarn over and draw through two loops on the hook. There should now be two loops on your hook.

02 Insert hook again

Without completing the stitch, yarn over and insert your hook into the next stitch. Draw up a loop, yarn over and draw through two loops on the hook. There should now be three loops on your hook.

03 And again

Repeat Step 02 into the next stitch. There should now be four loops on your hook, for three incomplete treble crochet stitches.

04 Pull through four

Yarn over and draw the yarn through all four loops on the hook to complete the decrease. Having worked into three stitches, but only created one, you have decreased your stitch count by two.

Post stitches

Add texture to your work by using post stitches, which can be worked both in front of and behind the previous row

Post stitches can be used to add texture to your work and, when worked in the correct pattern, they can create a distinctive ribbing effect. You can see how this stitch makes a good pattern to create ribbing on page 86 (post stitch rib). Usually post stitches are worked around treble crochets (tr) or bigger stitches, as double crochets (dc) aren't really tall enough to get your hook around. However, they can be done quite easily if that is what you want to do, so just follow this guide. It sees you insert your hook around the stitch rather than into the top V to create your next stitch. You can work by inserting your hook from front to back or from back to front, which creates a different visual depending on which side of the piece of crochet you're looking at.

Front post stitch

Insert your hook from front to back

01 Front to back to front

To work a front post treble crochet you need to yarn over (yo) then insert your hook into the gap between the posts of the row below from front to back, around the post next on the row and come through the other side back to the front of your work.

02 Draw up a loop

Yarn over and draw up a loop by pulling the working yarn back through to the right side of your crochet.

03 Complete your stitch

Now complete your stitch as usual.

Back post stitch

Insert your hook from back to front

> **TOP TIP**
> Post stitches can also be referred to as raised stitches or relief stitches, so look out for these phrases when you are looking at patterns.

01 Back to front to back

As the opposite to the front post stitch, you will take your hook to the back of your work, yarn over, and then insert your hook into the gap between posts coming from the back to the front, around the post and out of the back.

02 Yarn over and loop

Yarn over and draw up a loop back to where you started the stitch.

03 Complete your stitch

Now complete your stitch as normal.

Linked stitches

Close up the loose-looking stitches with this simple technique

Tall crochet stitches can end up looking quite loose, especially when the gaps between them are quite big. You can fix this by using linked stitches to close up the gaps. It helps create a solid fabric and produces a nice texture across them as well. You can apply linked stitches to anything taller than a double crochet (dc) by replacing the first yarn over(s) (yo) at the start of the stitch with a loop that links it to the previous stitch. It should be noted that you won't be counting the turning chain (t-ch) when you use this technique. Here we have used a linked treble crochet (ltr). It can be a little fiddly, but once you get the hang of it, like most crochet techniques, it's easy!

> "It can be a little fiddly, but once you get the hang of it, it's easy"

Linked stitches

Close gappy stitches

01 Foundation chain

Make a foundation chain for the number of stitches required in your pattern, then do an extra two chains. Insert your hook into the second chain from the hook, yarn over and draw up a loop. Insert your hook into the next chain, yarn over and draw up a loop. You will have three loops on your hook.

02 Do a treble

Now work the remainder of the stitch as a standard treble (tr) stitch. Yarn over, draw through two loops, yarn over, draw through two loops. You have now completed your first linked stitch. You will notice there is a horizontal bar half way up the stitch, this is where your next stitch will link to.

03 Top to bottom

Insert your hook into the horizontal bar from top to bottom.

04 Draw up a loop

Yarn over, draw up a loop (this replaces the yarn over at the start of a standard treble crochet). Insert your hook into the next chain.

05 Complete the treble

Now continue with the treble crochet. Yarn over, draw up a loop, (yarn over, and draw through two loops) twice. Repeat from Steps 03 to 05 until the end of the row.

06 Chain 2

To start a new row, chain two and turn your work. Insert the hook into the second chain from the hook, yarn over and draw up a loop. Insert your hook into the first stitch (at the base of the chain), and repeat Step 05 to complete the linked treble crochet.

07 Carry along the row

For each additional linked treble crochet, draw up a loop from the horizontal bar of the previous linked treble crochet. Insert your hook into the next stitch, as you would any other stitch. Now complete as you have done throughout the rest of the tutorial.

Link bigger stitches

You can use this technique to link taller stitches. Simply yarn over at the beginning of the stitch with a linked loop, and complete the stitch as usual. To link a double treble stitch (dtr), draw up a loop in the horizontal bar one- and two-thirds down the previous stitch (or the second and third chains of a chain three turning chain) to begin the stitch.

Joining

Finish projects that need joining together with these simple techniques

When making larger garments such as bags and items of clothing, a pattern can direct you to join pieces of crochet together. This is easy enough when it is simply attaching a motif, but when you are seaming together two separate parts of crochet, the process can become a touch more complicated, especially if you discover that the number of stitches do not correspond with each other.

When joining pieces you do so stitch by stitch to give a clean finish. Joining a piece worked in rows can be a little more complicated because of the difficulty of working into the row edges. If the number of stitches per row doesn't correspond then you may have to work more than one joining stitch into each V or row space. It is best when joining pieces of different sizes to place stitch markers along the pieces, holding them together every 5cm (2in) or so. This way you will be able to keep your stitches spaced more evenly.

Before you join your crochet, it is best to block your project's pieces first (if it's required). Otherwise you could experience a rippling effect later if you were to block them afterwards.

Whip stitch

Join your work simply

01 Hold 'wrong sides' together

Hold two pieces together with the wrong sides facing each other (the side of the pattern not meant to face the world). Pass your needle through the V stitches on both pieces from front to back and pull the yarn through.

02 Back to the front

Instead of doing your next stitch from back to front, simply draw your needle back to the front and repeat Step 01, inserting your needle from front to back. Repeat this until complete.

03 The finished look

Using a whip stitch will leave a visible line on both sides of the piece. This won't be quite as obvious when you are using the same colour yarn.

"Before you join your crochet, it is best to block your project's pieces first (if it's required)"

Mattress stitch

Make your join more secure

TOP TIP

Make sure you tie off your seaming yarn securely as if this comes undone the entire seam can unravel and you do not want that!

01 Lay them down

Lay your pieces side-by-side with the right sides facing you. Leaving a tail of 15cm (6in), insert your needle through the first edge stitch of the first piece and then down through the edge of the second.

02 Through stitch

Insert your needle down through the first stitch of piece one and up through to the second stitch.

03 Same to piece two

Now repeat the same process on piece two.

04 Repeat

Keep going up the edges of your two pieces. A loose 'ladder' will start to form. Stop when you have done about 2.5cm (1in).

05 Pull together

Now pull gently on the yarn so that the rungs of your ladder draw the two sides together. Be careful not to pull too tightly as this will make the crocheted pieces buckle.

06 Keep going

Repeat until you have reached the end, pulling the yarn to draw the edges together every 2.5cm (1in) or so. Notice how the seam is almost invisible. We've used a contrasting colour to make it obvious, but when it is the same colour you'll barely know it's there!

Slip stitch

Crochet your pieces together

01 Slip stitch (sl st)

Insert your hook through the first stitch on both pieces of crochet. Complete your slip stitch (or double crochet) along the edge.

02 Keep going

Now keep going, ensuring you match up the stitches as you go.

Slip stitch

A slip stitch seam is strong, and will be almost invisible from the other side of the work. Be mindful that slip stitches do not allow for any give, so making them too tight will pucker the fabric. Keep your tension loose but secure.

Double crochet

Using a double crochet will give a more pronounced edge, but this can be used to your advantage if you want a decorative seam. It is also stretchier than a slip stitch join.

Flat slip-stitched seam

Make a flat and symmetrical join

01 Top to bottom

Insert your hook from top to bottom through the back loop only on the right-hand piece of fabric.

02 Now to the left

Do the same on your left piece, then yarn over (yo) and pull through both loops on the hook. Repeat until you reach the end.

Flat slip-stitched seam

This seam produces a flat row of chain-looking stitches. It's a neat finish and adds a nice little detail to your seams.

"It is best when joining pieces of different sizes to place stitch markers along the pieces, holding them together every 5cm (2in) or so"

Check the name

Each of the stitches used here has another name, so it is best to be aware of these just in case the pattern you are using calls them by another name:

- Whip stitch: overcast stitch
- Mattress stitch: ladder stitch
- Slip stitch: double crochet seam

Going Further

Master all of these stitches and take your projects to the next level

Granny squares

Create the most recognisable crochet pattern in the world: the granny square!

Granny square

Make the first square in a project

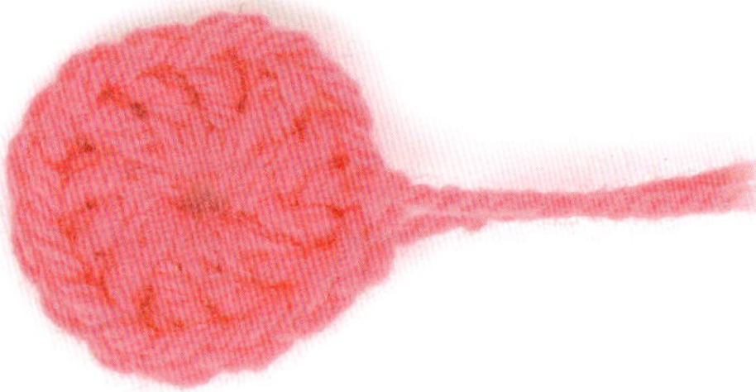

01 Round 1

Make a magic ring (or chain 4 and join with a sl st into a ring).
Round 1: Ch 3 (counts as a tr here and throughout). Working into the ring, 2 tr, ch 1, (3 tr, ch 1) 3 times. Pull your magic ring closed gently. Join with a sl st into the stop of the chain 3 and fasten off.

02 Round 2

Fasten on with your next yarn into any ch-sp. Ch 3, (2 tr, ch 1, 3 tr) in chain ch-sp, ch 1, (3 tr, ch 1, 3 tr, ch 1) into next 3 ch-sp. Join with sl st to top of ch 3. Fasten off.

03 Round 3

Fasten on with next yarn at any edge ch-sp. Ch 3, 2 tr in same ch-sp. Ch 1, *(3 tr, ch 1, 3 tr, ch 1) in next corner ch-sp. 3 dc in next edge ch-sp, ch 1. Repeat from * twice more. (3 tr, ch 1, 3 tr, ch 1) in last corner ch-sp. Join with sl st to top of ch 3. Fasten off.

04 All future rounds

For all further rounds, fasten on at any edge ch-sp. Ch 3, 2 tr in same ch-sp, ch 1. Make (3 tr, ch 1) in each edge space, and repeat (3 tr, ch 1) twice in each corner space. Join with a sl st into top of ch 3.

TOP TIP

Create as many granny squares as you want and join them together with a stitch of your choice (see page 38). It makes a brilliant blanket and it is an absolute classic!

Granny triangles

Drop a corner and add an extra stitch to each cluster to create a triangle

Did you know?

It is slightly harder to make a straight blanket out of triangles, but you can make up hexagons out of six triangles and then join each hexagon together with two triangles. You can use a connecting stitch of your choice, simply refer to page 38 for joining guidance. Remember, this won't give you a straight edge — but who needs a straight edge, really?

Granny triangle

Make a variant of the granny square

01 Round 1

Make a magic ring (or chain 4 and join with a sl st into a ring).
Round 1: Ch 3 (counts as a tr here and throughout). Working into the ring, 3 tr, ch 2, (4 tr, ch 2) 2 times. Pull your magic ring closed gently. Join with a sl st into the top of the chain 3 and fasten off.

02 Round 2

Fasten on with your next yarn into any ch-sp. Ch 3, (3 tr, ch 2, 4 tr) in chain ch-sp, ch 1, (4 tr, ch 2, 4 tr, ch 2) into next 3 ch-sp. Join with sl st to top of ch 3. Fasten off.

03 Round 3

Fasten on with next yarn at any edge ch-sp. Ch 3, 3 tr in same ch-sp. Ch 1, *(4 tr, ch 2, 4 tr, ch 2) in next corner ch-sp. 4 tr in next edge ch-sp, ch 1. Repeat from * once more. (4 tr, ch 2, 4 tr, ch 2) in last corner ch-sp. Join with sl st to top of ch 3. Fasten off.

04 All future rounds

For all further rounds:
Fasten on at any edge ch-sp. Ch 3, 3 tr in same ch-sp, ch 2. Make (4 tr, ch 2) in each edge space, and repeat (4 tr, ch 2) twice in each corner space. Join with a sl st into top of ch 3.

Granny stripes

Don't want to make granny squares and stitch them together? Try the same pattern, just in rows instead!

01 Foundation

Chain a multiple of 3, plus an extra 4.

02 Row 1

Work 3 treble crochet into the 7th chain from your hook. Chain 1, skip 2 chains, then work 3 treble crochets into the next chain; repeat this across the row until there are 3 unworked chains left. Chain 1 and work 1 treble crochet into the final chain.

03 Row 2

Chain 3 (this counts as a treble crochet) and turn your work. Place 1 treble crochet in the chain space. Chain 1, then work 3 treble crochets into the next chain space; repeat this to the end of the row, finishing with 1 chain and 2 treble crochets in your turning chain.

04 Row 3

Chain 4 (this counts as 1 treble crochet and 1 chain) and turn. Work 3 treble crochets into the next chain space, then chain 1; repeat this to the end of the row, finishing with 1 treble crochet into your turning chain.

TOP TIP

Not sure what colours to use or how many rows you should crochet of each? There are plenty of resources online at places like randomstripes.com and biscuitsandjam.com/stripe_maker.php

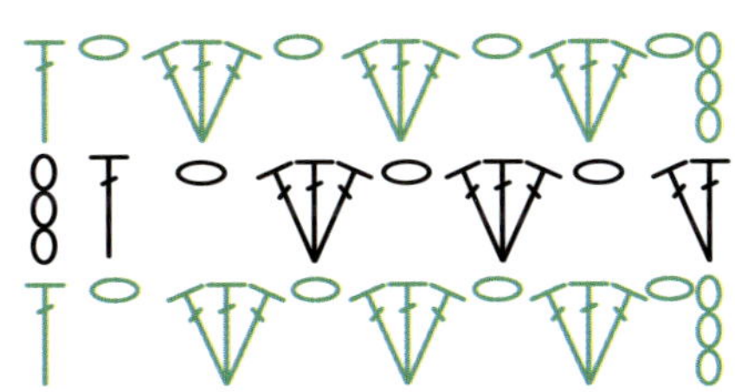

05 Building it up

Repeat Steps 03 and 04 to create the pattern.

Corner to corner

This stitch is exactly what it sounds like — you start in one corner of the project and finish in the opposite corner using increases and decreases. Don't worry, we've got you covered with tutorials for both!

Increasing

01 The first corner

Chain six, then work treble crochet in each of the fourth, fifth and sixth chains from your hook — this makes your first corner.

02 Starting the next row

Turn your work and repeat Step 01, then slip stitch into the turning chain of the previous row. This is an increase — you've just created the first block in your second row. This is how you will start each row.

03 Working the second row

Chain three and then work three triple crochets into the turning chain you just slip stitched into, then slip stitch into the turning chain of the previous blocks. Repeat this step to finish the diagonal row.

04 Building blocks

Keep making new rows of blocks until you reach your desired length.

Decreasing

01 Making it smaller

Once you've increased all you need to, it's time to decrease. Turn your work and slip stitch across the three treble crochets so that you're at the other side of your last square.

02 Working the rows

Chain three and then treble crochet into three triple crochets into the turning chains of the previous block. Slip stitch into the previous turning chain. Repeat this until you reach the end of the row. You should have one less square than the previous row.

03 Finishing off

Turn your work and repeat Steps 01 and 02. Keep going until you're down to a single square, just like your first increasing row.

Understanding charts

Corner to corner (or C2C) patterns will sometimes be written out like normal ones, but you could also be presented with a graph. So how do you read it? It's actually more straightforward than you think.

Each square on the graph or chart represents a stitch. Start in the bottom-right corner and follow the chart complete with colour changes, crossing off your diagonal rows as you go to keep track. But make sure you count how many squares you need of each colour in a row — you don't want to notice a mistake too late and have to start frogging everything!

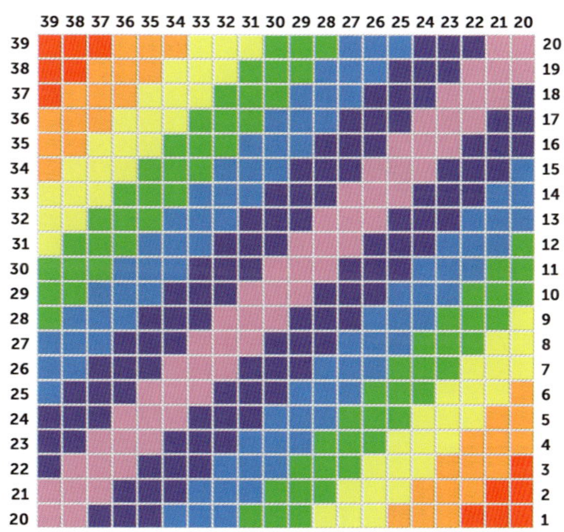

TOP TIP

If you want to take this stitch further, try introducing some colour changes. Adding a border to your work will neaten up any wonky edges. For border ideas, turn to page 112.

Herringbone

While it might sound fancy, this stitch is actually quite easy.

Herringbone is incredibly similar to treble crochet, just with a slight twist, so it's perfect for beginners looking to take the next step. One of the best things about herringbone is how versatile it is; you can whip up amazing blankets and cushions, as well as wearables like scarves and shawls. It also has the added advantage that because it is just a variation of treble crochet, you can increase and decrease as you normally would. Why not have a go? Stitch is also known as Herringbone treble crochet (UK), and Herringbone double crochet (US).

01 Foundation

Chain as many as you want, and then add 2 more chains. Yarn over and insert your hook into the 3rd chain from your hook.

02 Start the stitch

Yarn over and pull through the chain and first loop on your hook.

03 Keep going

Yarn over and pull through the next loop on your hook.

04 The last bit

Finally, yarn over and pull through both loops left on your hook. Repeat across the row, working 1 herringbone treble in each chain to the end.

05 Repeat

Chain 2 and turn, work 1 herringbone treble into next and every following stitch to end, working last stitch into top of turning chain. At the end of each row, chain two and turn — this will be your turning chain and doesn't count as a stitch. Then make a herringbone stitch in every stitch across.

TOP TIP

If you find the edges of your work getting wavy, try ending each row with a treble crochet instead of a herringbone stitch.

Mixed grit stitch

While it works up slowly, the mixed grit stitch creates a dense fabric, making it perfect for scarves to keep out the chill on those cold winter days. It can also make for some stunning blankets, although patience is key as they may take a while to make!

01 Foundation

Chain an odd number.

03 Row 2

Chain 2 and turn your work. Skip the 1st stitch, then *work 1 double crochet and 1 treble crochet into the next stitch, skip the next stitch: repeat from * to the end of the last stitch, then finish with 1 double crochet in this stitch.

02 Row 1

Work a double crochet into the 2nd chain from your hook, and then into each chain across.

04 Row 3

Chain 2 and turn your work. Work 1 double crochet and 1 treble crochet into every treble crochet across, finishing with a double crochet in the top of your turning chain.

05 Repeat

Repeat Step 04 to create the pattern.

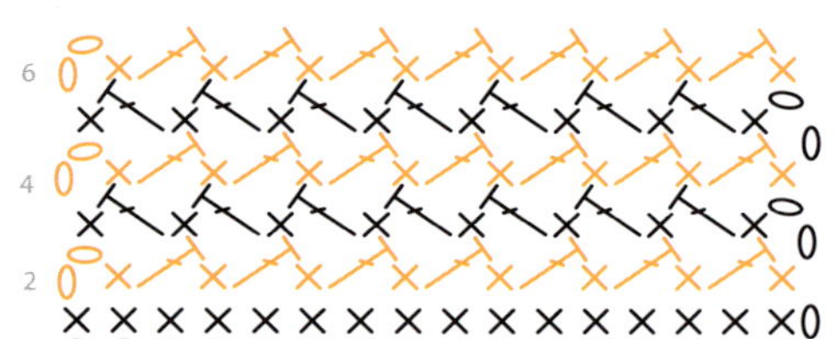

Granite

Looking for an easy way to create great texture? Comprising chains, skips and double crochets, granite stitch is everything you're looking for, and it can be used in so many different projects, from blankets and scarves to washcloths and sweaters.

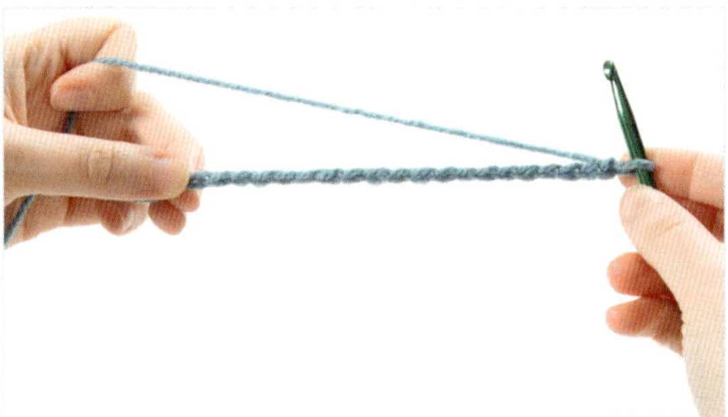

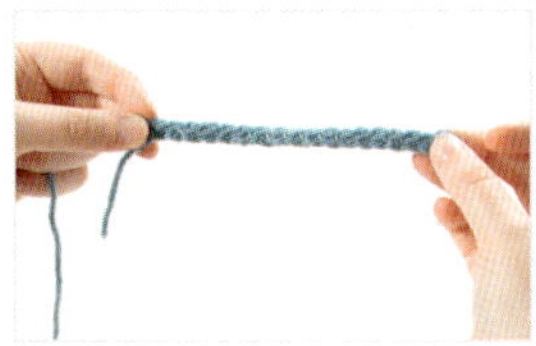

01 Foundation & row 1

Chain an even number, then make 1 double crochet into the 2nd chain from the hook and in every chain across. Chain 1 and turn your work then move to row 2.

02 Row 2

Chain 1 and work 1 double crochet in the next stitch. Chain 1 and skip the next stitch, then work a double crochet in the following stitch. Repeat this until the last stitch, work a double crochet in this stitch.

03 Do it again

Repeat Step 02 until your work reaches your desired length. That's all there is to it!

TOP TIP

Pay attention to your counting when learning this stitch!

Waistcoat stitch

If you're looking to bring a little knit to your crochet, this is the stitch for you. Also known as: Centre double crochet; knit stitch.

01 Foundation

Chain until you reach the desired width for your project.

02 Row 1

In the 2nd chain from your hook, work 1 double crochet, then double crochet in each chain across the row.

TOP TIP Try going up a hook size — you'll find it much easier to work your way through the stitches.

03 Row 2

Chain 1 and turn your work. Work 1 double crochet into the next stitch, but by putting your hook through the middle of the body of the stitch below rather than under the V. Continue this across the row.

04 Keep going

Repeat Step 03 to continue the pattern.

Lemon peel stitch

The texture made from this stitch is gorgeous, and the best part? Doing it is easy peasy. Comprising just double and treble crochets, you'll be working up your beanies, scarves, washcloths and more in no time at all. Also known as the Up-and-down stitch.

01 Foundation

Chain an odd number.

02 Row 1

Work 1 double crochet into the 2nd chain from your hook. Then *make 1 treble crochet in the next chain, 1 double crochet in the next chain, and repeat from * to the end. You should finish with 1 treble crochet in the last chain.

TOP TIP

Make sure to count your rows as you go along — it can be quite hard to go back and count them with this stitch!

03 Row 2

Chain 1 and turn your work. *Work 1 double crochet into the next stitch then 1 treble crochet into the next stitch; repeat from * to the end.

04 Do it again

Repeat Step 03 for the pattern.

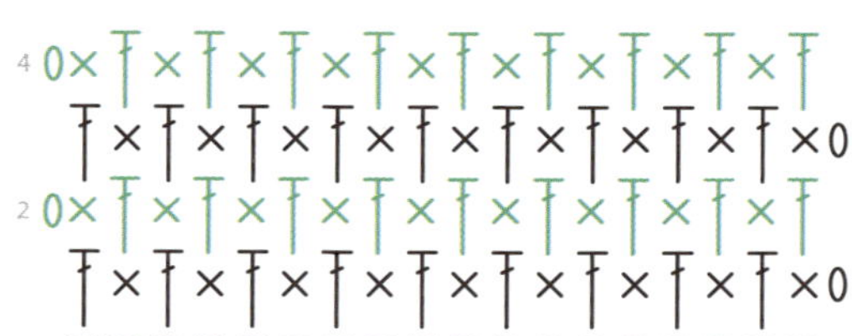

Filet squares

This is a wonderful technique that allows you to spell words, make motifs and so much more, all by using empty space. Here we'll teach you the basic version — once you've mastered this, you can experiment to create your own designs.

01 Foundation

Chain a multiple of 6, plus an extra 3.

03 Row 2

Chain 3 and turn — this counts as a treble crochet. Work 2 treble crochets into the next chain-2 space, 1 treble crochet into the next stitch, chain 2 and then skip 2 stitches. Work 1 treble crochet into the next stitch, 2 treble crochets into the next chain-2 space, 1 treble crochet in the next stitch, chain 2 and skip the next 2 stitches; repeat this to the end of the row, finishing with 1 treble crochet in the top of your turning chain from the previous row.

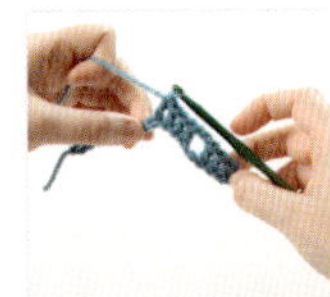

02 Row 1

Work 1 treble crochet into the 4th chain from your hook, then 1 treble crochet in each of the next 2 chains. Chain 2 and skip the next 2 chains. Work 1 treble crochet into the next 4 chains, chain 2, skip 2; repeat this across to the last chain, working 1 treble crochet into it.

04 Keep going

Repeat Step 03 to create the pattern.

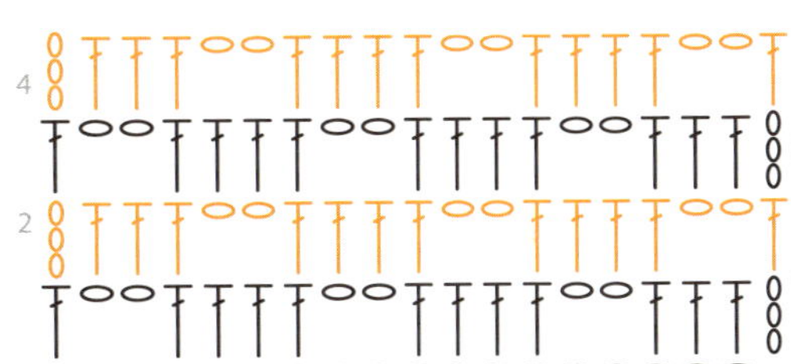

Ripple stitch

To create a wave effect, all you have to use are increases and decreases; alternating them at certain points will make the peaks and troughs that are so characteristic of the ripple and chevron. One of the great things about this stitch is its versatility — it can be used for blankets, scarves and washcloths.

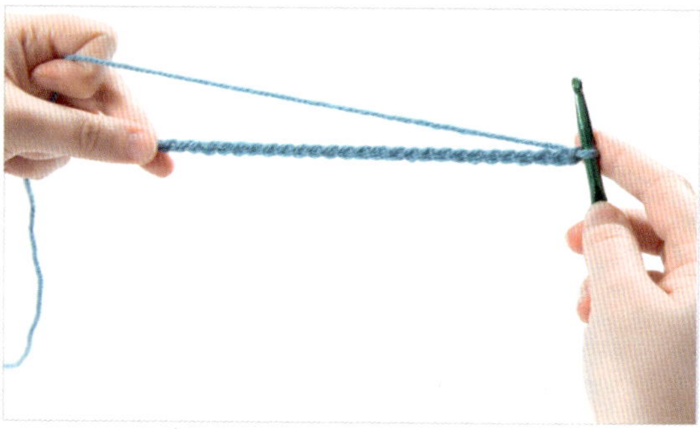

01 Foundation

Chain a multiple of 12, plus 3.

02 Get started

Work a treble crochet into the 4th chain from your hook, then another treble crochet in each of the next 3 chains. Treble 2 together twice.

03 Finish the row

Work 1 treble crochet into each of the next 3 chains, work 2 treble crochets into each of the next 2 chains, work a treble crochet into the next 3 chains, then treble 2 together twice; repeat this across until you have 4 unworked chains left. Work 1 treble crochet into each of the next 3 chains, then work 2 treble crochets into the last one.

TOP TIP

Are you after points rather than waves? Only make one increase and decrease instead of two to make a chevron.

04 Starting row 2

Chain 3 (this counts as a treble crochet) and turn your work. Work another treble crochet into the same stitch, work 1 treble crochet into each of the next 3 stitches, then treble 2 together twice.

05 Finishing row 2

Work 1 treble crochet into the next 3 stitches, work 2 treble crochets into each of the next 2 stitches, 1 treble crochet into each of the next 3 stitches, then treble 2 together twice; repeat this across until there are 3 unworked stitches and the turning chain left. Work 1 treble crochet into the next 3 stitches, then finish with 2 treble crochets in the top of your turning chain.

06 Make some waves

Repeat Steps 04 and 05 to create the pattern.

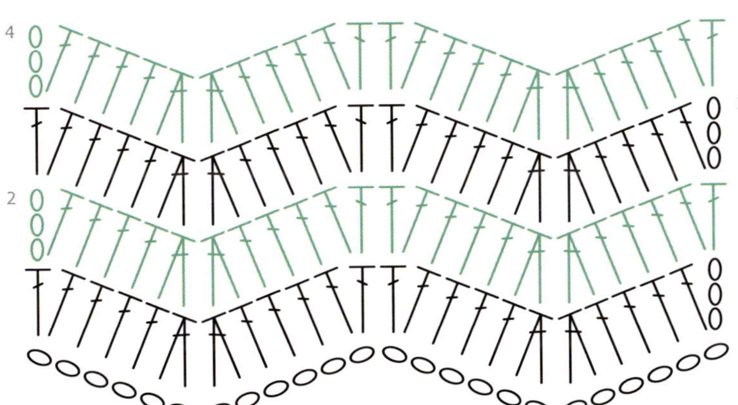

Shells, fans and V stitches

Create better edges with these three decorative embellishments

In crochet, the terms shell and fan are used interchangeably, but in actual fact they are not quite the same. Where a shell sees you use a solid run of stitches, a fan will utilise the added gap of a chain space (ch-sp). Meanwhile, the V stitch uses fewer stitches, and comprises two stitches in the same stitch, separated by a chain. The result is a singular chain space. Shells and fans typically use five stitches into the same stitch. They are best used with treble (tr) or double treble (dtr) stitches as this makes them more prominent.

Below are some examples of how each of these would be worked, and what the end product would look like.

"Where a shell sees you use a solid run of stitches, a fan will utilise the added gap of a chain space"

Shell

Skip the next stitch, 5 treble into next stitch, skip stitch, continue with pattern.

Fan

Skip the next stitch, (treble, chain (ch) 1, treble, chain 1, treble) into next stitch, skip stitch, continue with pattern.

V stitch

Skip the next stitch, (treble, chain 1, treble) into next stitch, skip stitch, continue with pattern.

V bobbles

So you've mastered the bobble stitch (although there's a reminder below in case you've forgotten) — now it's time to take it further. The best part is that while it may sound complicated, it's really anything but.

Bobble - (Yarn over, insert hook into stitch and draw up a loop, yarn over and draw through 2 loops on hook) twice, then yarn over and draw through all 3 loops on your hook.

V bobble - (Bobble, chain 1, bobble) in specified stitch.

01 Foundation

Chain a multiple of 4, and then another 3.

03 Row 2

Chain 3 (this counts as a treble crochet) and turn your work. Work a V bobble into the top of the last V bobble in the previous row. *Work 1 treble crochet into the next stitch, 1 V bobble in the top of the V bobble from the previous row; repeat from * to the last stitch, finishing with a treble crochet in the top of the turning chain.

02 Row 1

Make a V bobble in the 5th chain from your hook, then skip the next chain. *Work 1 treble crochet into the next chain, skip 1 chain, V bobble in the next chain, then skip 1 chain; repeat from* until there's 1 unworked chain left. Work 1 treble crochet into the last chain.

04 Do it again

Repeat Step 03 for the pattern.

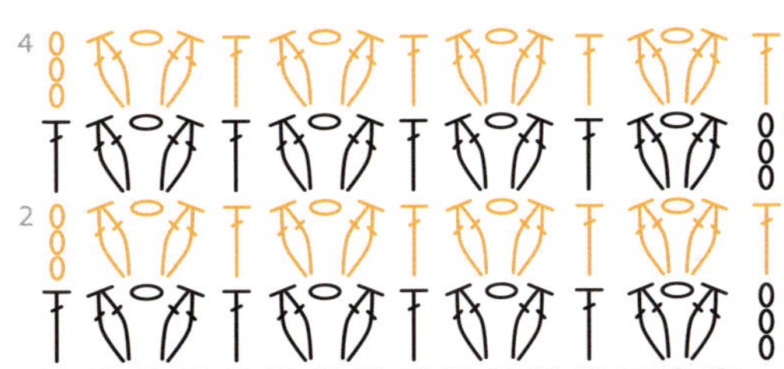

Diamond fans

For something unique, why not try your hand at some diamond fans? They're perfect to add some individuality to scarves and blankets.

V stitch - (1 treble crochet, 1 chain, 1 treble crochet) into a specified stitch.

01 Foundation

Chain a multiple of 4, plus an extra 2.

02 Row 1

Work 1 double crochet into the 2nd chain from your hook. Chain 5, skip the next 3 chains, then work 1 double crochet into the next chain; repeat across the row.

03 Row 2

Chain 3 (this counts as a treble crochet) and turn. Work 1 treble crochet into the same stitch and chain 1. Work 1 double crochet into the next chain-5 space, chain 1, work a V stitch into the next double crochet and chain 1; repeat this across to the last chain-5 space. Work 1 double crochet into the last chain-5 space, chain 1, and work 2 treble crochets in the last stitch.

04 Row 4

Chain 1 and turn your work. Work 1 double crochet in the next stitch and chain 5. Work 1 double crochet into the top of the V stitch below, chain 5 and repeat this across to the end of the row, finishing with 1 double crochet in the top of the turning chain.

05 Keep going

Repeat Steps 03 and 04 to make the pattern.

Diamond overlay

Make your blankets stand out with this unique stitch.

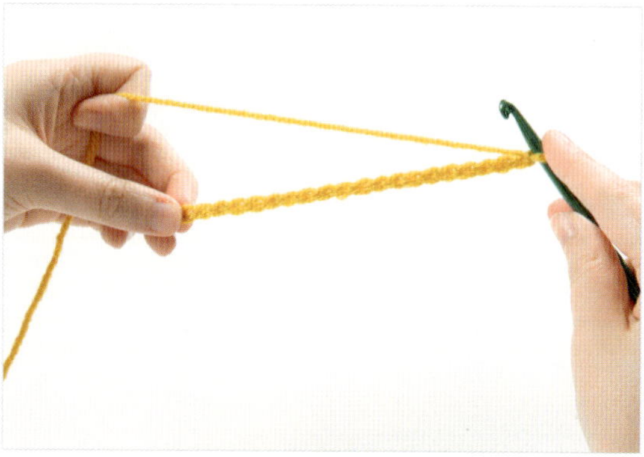

01 Foundation

Chain a multiple of 6, plus an extra 3.

02 Row 1

Work 1 double crochet into the 2nd chain from your hook, then in every remaining chain across.

03 Row 2

Chain 3 (this counts as a treble crochet) and turn. Skip the next 2 stitches, work 1 double treble crochet into the next stitch, then work 1 treble crochet in each of the 2 skipped stitches (working behind the stitch you've just made), skip 1 stitch, work 1 treble in each of the next 2 stitches, work 1 double treble into the skipped stitch (working in front of the trebles you've just made); repeat this across to the last stitch. Work 1 treble crochet into the last stitch.

04 Row 3

Chain 1, turn your work, and place 1 double crochet in each stitch across.

05 Row 4

Chain 3 and turn. Skip the next stitch, place 1 treble crochet in the next one, then work 1 double treble crochet into the skipped stitch (working in front of the stitch you just made), skip the next 2 stitches, work 1 double treble crochet into the next stitch, then 1 treble crochet in each of the skipped stitches (working behind the stitch you just made); repeat this across to the last stitch. Work 1 treble crochet into the last stitch.

06 Row 5

Chain 1, turn your work, and work 1 double crochet in each stitch across.

07 Keep building

Repeat Steps 03-06 to create the pattern.

Offset arches

A mix of shells and V stitches, offset arches are great for pretty much everything, but they can be a little challenging. Counting is key here — make sure you've made enough treble crochets in your shells, and keep track of your chains!

Shell - Work 4 treble crochets, 1 chain and 4 more treble crochets into the specified stitch.

V stitch - Work 1 treble crochet, 1 chain and another treble crochet into the specified stitch.

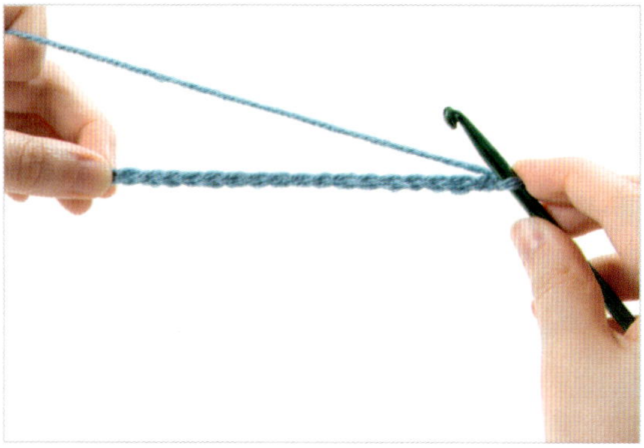

01 Foundation

Chain a multiple of 8, plus an extra 2.

02 Row 1

Work 1 double crochet into the 2nd chain from your hook. Skip the next 3 chains, make 1 shell in the next chain, skip 3 chains, then work 1 double crochet into the next chain; repeat this to the end of the row.

03 Row 2

Chain 3 (this counts as a stitch), turn, work 1 treble crochet into the same stitch and chain 2. *Work 1 double crochet into the top of the next shell, chain 2, work 1 V stitch in the next double crochet, then chain 2; repeat from * across to the last shell. Work a double crochet into the top of the last shell, chain 2, then place 2 treble crochets in the last stitch.

05 Row 4

Chain 1 and turn, then work a double crochet into the first treble stitch and chain 2. *Work a V stitch into the next double crochet, chain 2, work a double crochet into the top of the next shell, then chain 2; repeat from * to the last double crochet. In this stitch, work a V stitch, chain 2 and work a double crochet into the top of the turning chain.

07 Keep going

Repeat Steps 03-06 to create the pattern.

04 Row 3

Chain 3 and turn, then work 4 treble crochets into the same stitch. *Work 1 double crochet in the next double crochet stitch, then a shell in the top of the next V stitch; repeat from * across to the last double crochet. Work a double crochet into that stitch, then place 5 treble crochets in the top of the turning chain.

06 Row 5

Chain 1 and turn, then work a double crochet into the next stitch. Work a shell in the top of the next V stitch, then double crochet in the next double crochet; repeat this across to the end of the row.

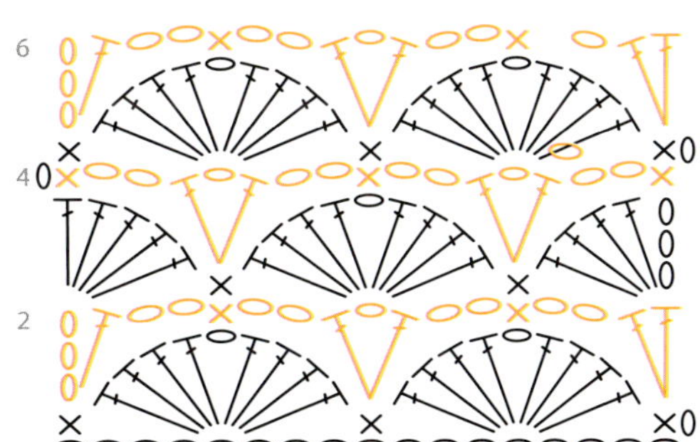

Chain mesh

Perfect for everything from blankets and sweaters to market bags, chain mesh is a great way to give your work some style. Best of all, the open and lacy pattern is easy to make using a simple combination of double crochets and chains.

01 Foundation

Chain a multiple of four, and then add an extra two chains on the end.

02 Row 1

Work a double crochet into the 2nd chain from your hook. Next, chain 5, skip the next 3 chains, and work a double crochet in the next chain. Repeat this until the end of the row.

03 Row 2

Chain 5 (this counts as a treble crochet plus 2 chains) and turn. Work one double crochet in the next chain-5 space, chain 5, then work another double crochet in the next chain-5 space. Repeat the chains and double crochets until the last chain-5 space has been worked, then chain 2 and work a treble crochet in the double crochet at the end of the row.

04 Row 3

Chain 1 and turn. Work a double crochet into the next stitch and then chain 5. Work a double crochet in the next chain-5 space, chain 5 and repeat this across to the end of the row, working a double crochet in the 3rd chain of your turning chain.

05 Keep going

Repeat Steps 03 and 04 to make the pattern.

06 A neat finish

To create a straight edge along the top of your work, chain 4 at the end of Step 04 (this counts as a half treble crochet plus 2 chains) and turn. Work one double crochet in the next chain-5 space, chain 3, then work another double crochet in the next chain-5 space. Repeat the chains and double crochets until the last chain-5 space has been worked into, chain 2 and work a half treble crochet into the last stitch.

Blocking

When working with an open, lacy stitch like chain mesh, blocking is important to really define the arches. If you've never blocked anything before, don't worry — it's quite straightforward.

Pin your work to a blocking mat (or another flat, padded surface). Be sure to use rust-proof pins to avoid staining your yarn, and space the pins evenly to create nice flat edges. Now that everything's in place, you can either spray your work with an even coat of water or steam it with a steamer or iron. Next, pat the surface gently to help the water absorb into the fibres and then leave it to dry.

It's best to leave your project to dry for 24 hours or more if possible until completely dry. The rate at which it dries depends on the room temperature, the type of yarn used and how much moisture was retained in the fibres.

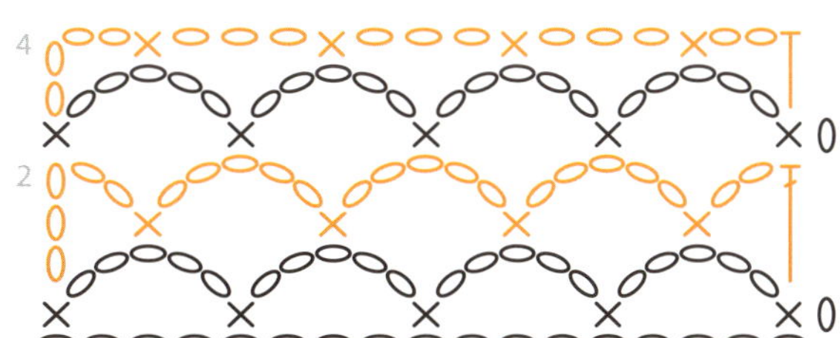

Mini picot mesh

A stylish variant of the straightforward mesh, this stitch uses picots for added detail. Consisting of a two-row repeat, it's great for beginners and can be worked up pretty fast to create stunning blankets and market bags.

Picot - chain 3, insert your hook into the 3rd chain from your hook, yarn over and draw through.

01 Foundation

Chain a multiple of 3, plus an extra 2.

02 Row 1

Work a double crochet into the 2nd chain from your hook. *Chain 3, skip the next 2 chains, work 1 double crochet into the next chain, make a picot; repeat from * until you reach the last 3 chains in your foundation. Here, chain 3, skip the next 2 chains, and work a double crochet into the last one.

TOP TIP

Blocking is always essential with lacy, open patterns like this.

03 Row 2

Chain 4 and turn (counts as 1 treble and 1 chain). *Work a double crochet into the next chain-3 space, make a picot and chain 3; repeat from * to the last chain-3 space, then make a double crochet in the last chain-3 space, picot, chain 1 and work a treble crochet into the last stitch.

04 Row 3

Chain 1 and turn. Work a double crochet into the first stitch and chain 3. *Make a double crochet in the next chain-3 space, picot, chain 3; repeat from * to the end, finishing with a double crochet in the 3rd chain of your turning chain.

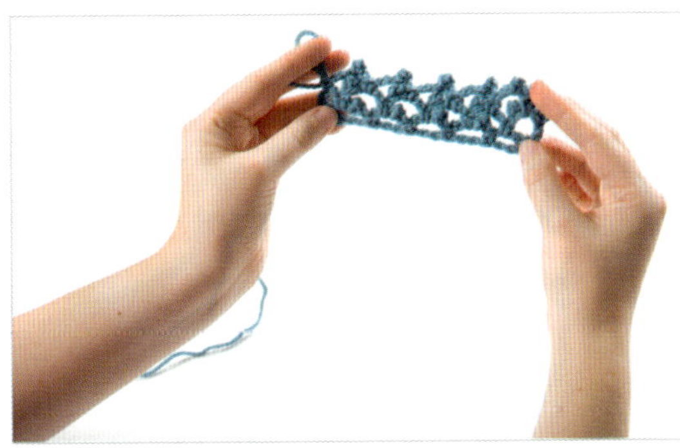

05 Expand your mesh

Repeat Steps 03 and 04 for the pattern. To give a straighter edge at the end, omit the picots from the final row.

Broomstick lace

Traditionally made with the handle of a broomstick, hence the name, here we've used a 20mm knitting needle to create a stitch that will catch everyone's eye.

01 Foundation

Your starting chain should be as many loops as you want for your pattern, plus 1 extra for your turning chain. Here we've chained 20, plus the extra 1.

02 Row 1

Work 1 double crochet into the 2nd chain from your hook, and in each chain across.

03 The first loop

Insert your crochet hook into the 1st double crochet on the left side of the row. Yarn over and draw up a loop, then slide the loop onto your stick. Here we've used a 20mm knitting needle.

TOP TIP
Here we've crocheted 5 clusters of 4 loops each, but you can alter your foundation chain to meet your needs.

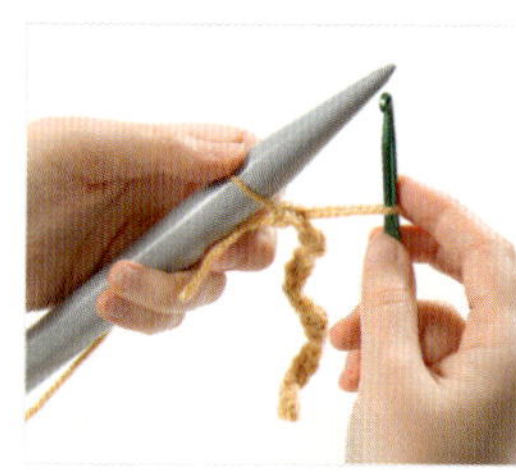

04 The rest of the row

Remove your hook and insert it into the next double crochet. Yarn over, pull up a loop and slide it onto your stick. Repeat this across the row.

05 Making your clusters

Slide the last 4 loops you made off your stick and insert your hook from right to left. Yarn over and pull through all four loops, then chain 1 for your turning chain. Make 4 double crochets in the cluster (the number of stitches equals the number of loops in the cluster). Repeat this across the row, minus the turning chain.

06 Row 3

Chain 1 and turn. Work 1 double crochet into every stitch across.

07 Keep going

Repeat Steps 04-06 to create the pattern.

Wattle stitch

Perfect for baby blankets, scarves, washcloths and more, this simple stitch brings a homely feel.

01 Foundation

Chain a multiple of 3.

02 Row 1

In the 3rd chain from your hook, work 1 double crochet, 1 chain and another double crochet. * Skip 2 chains, work 1 double crochet, 1 chain and another double crochet all in the next chain; repeat from * across the row, finishing with just 1 double crochet in the last chain.

03 Row 2

Chain 1 and turn your work. Work 1 double crochet, 1 chain and another double crochet into every chain space across, finishing with 1 double crochet in the turning chain.

TOP TIP If you're struggling to find those chain spaces, try stretching your work a little and you should be able to spot them more easily.

04 Keep going

Repeat Step 03 for the pattern.

Spike stitches

Add texture and detail to your piece with the simple spike stitch

One of the best things about crochet is that you don't have to do much in order to add an extra little flourish to your work. It's easy to work up a different type of stitch, change colour or add a motif. A spike stitch is a good example of a really simple way to add detail to your crochet projects, and doesn't take too much work to incorporate.

Adding spike stitches in the same colour is a great way of adding subtle texture to your work, and using a contrasting colour is perfect for adding a statement to your projects. Put simply, a spike stitch is one that extends down more than a single row. You form it by going into the usual V space, but on rows that you have already worked. It forms a longer version of the stitch.

To really add some extra flavour to your work, you could mix spike stitches with crossed stitches, working in the stitch ahead before coming back into the previous stitch. In this following tutorial we will show you have to do the most simple spike stitches.

Spike stitches

Add a flourish to your work

TOP TIP
Spike stitches are also known as long stitches and dropped stitches.

01 Insert your hook

Work your next stitch as usual, but insert your hook into the space however many rows beneath your current row as you desire. Here we have chosen one row beneath.

02 Draw up a loop

Bring the yarn over your hook, then pull it back through and draw up a loop to the height of your current row so that it looks level.

03 Complete your stitch

Now complete the stitch as usual. Yarn over (yo) and pull it through all loops on the hook.

Different lengths

These spike stitches are worked into different rows in a contrasting colour. Here we have used the following pattern: *spike stitch into stitch 1 row below, double crochet (dc) in next st, spike into stitch 2 rows below, double crochet in next stitch; repeat from * to end.

Crossed stitches

Give your crochet a more detailed and advanced look with a really simple method

Adding detail to your crochet doesn't need to be difficult, feel like a chore or take too long. In fact, adding a varied stitch during your rows can do a lot to make your work look more interesting, and make it look more impressive than a simple flat piece of crochet.

A crossed stitch really isn't too difficult and can be used with great effect to produce a cable-like look to your projects. You can pair them with multiple other stitches to create a pretty effect that you might not have thought possible due to the simplicity of crochet.

There are three different ways in which you can work a crossed stitch. You can either work the second stitch in front or behind the one before it, or you can wrap it around the first stitch. Patterns may not specify which method you should use, but usually it will reference which option to adopt in the instructions. You will generally be able to follow written out, clear instructions.

All crossed stitches are formed by skipping the next stitch, crocheting into the second stitch from your hook and then going back into the stitch that you missed.

> "Take time to identify the stitches and work carefully to make sure your crossed stitches come out well, especially if working several crossed stitches at once to create a cable effect."

Did you know?
James Buchanan, US president between 1857 and 1861 liked to crochet in his free time.

Cross behind
The first option

01 Skip a stitch
Skip the next stitch from where you have been working, and then locate the stitch you skipped — this is where you will work next.

02 Tilt your stitches
Either tilt your work forward or hold down the previous stitch with your thumb while you insert the hook, working behind the first stitch.

03 Complete the cross
Yarn over (yo) your inserted hook, then complete your stitch as required. That's it!

Cross in front

A similar process

01 Skip the stitch
As with working behind, skip the next stitch from where you have been working, then locate the stitch you skipped. This is where you will work next.

02 Push back
This time, instead of tilting your work forward to work behind it, push it back so you can complete the stitch into the skipped stitch from the front.

03 Complete the stitch
Insert your hook into the skip stitch and then complete the stitch as you would usually.

Wrapped

The third and final option

01 Yarn over
Yarn over and insert your hook into the skipped stitch, working in front of the previous stitch.

02 Yarn to the back
With the yarn at the back of your work, yarn over and draw up a loop, bring the loop around the front of the first stitch.

03 Complete the stitch
Complete the stitch as usual. The second stitch will enclose the base of the first one.

Cluster stitches

Join any number of stitches together to form a cluster

Cluster stitches is a term that can be used to define several different types of collected stitches, but the most basic type is several incomplete stitches that are joined together at the top to form a triangle. Cluster stitches can be used as decreases, and can form patterns when used with a combination of other stitches and chains.

There are no strict rules to follow when it comes to the number of stitches you can use in your cluster, and you can use any long sort of stitch. The pattern you are using will specify what combination of stitches should be used for that pattern, and will never simply define it as a cluster. In this tutorial we will teach you how to do a basic four-treble cluster (4-tr) stitch.

"There are no strict rules to follow when it comes to the number of stitches you can use in your cluster, and you can use any long sort of stitch"

Cluster stitch

Form a four-treble cluster stitch

01 Start your cluster

Yarn over (yo) your hook, insert the tip into the next stitch and draw up a loop.

02 Continue the treble (tr)

Yarn over your hook again and draw the yarn through two loops on the hook. Leave the remaining two loops on the hook!

03 Repeat

Rather than completing the treble crochet, you will yarn over your hook and insert it into the next stitch before drawing up another loop.

04 Keep going

Rather than completing the treble crochet, you will yarn over your hook and insert it into the next stitch before drawing up another loop.

05 Repeat twice more

Now repeat Steps 03 and 04 twice. You will end up with five loops left on your hook and half-completed four stitches.

06 Through the loops

Yarn over and draw the yarn through all five loops on the hook. This completes your cluster.

Not a bobble...

The cluster stitch is not to be confused with the bobble stitch, which is often referred to by the same name but the end result will be altogether different.

Puff stitches

Use puff stitches to create a reversible, cushioned fabric using half treble crochet stitches

Puff stitches are some of the most unusual crochet stitches you will come across. They don't involve the usual method of completing a stitch every two loops. Instead, a puff stitch sees you draw up loops to the height of the other stitches and secure these longer, puffed-out pieces of yarn with a stitch at the top. Puff stitches look identical on either side and work brilliantly for projects such as blankets and coasters, when you want them to work either way up. Puff stitches can take a little while to get used to, but just make sure you work them loosely, and you'll get the hang of it in no time at all.

> "Puff stitches look identical on either side and work brilliantly for projects such as blankets and coasters"

Puff stitch

Create a reversible stitch

01 Start the puff stitch

Yarn over (yo) and insert your hook into the next stitch. Draw up a loop. You should have three loops on your hook. Do not pull the working yarn through any of the loops.

02 Draw up

Careful not to pull on the stitch you have worked into, pull the loop up to the desired height. Level it with the height of the other worked stitches. Do not pull too tightly and let the yarn lie quite loosely.

03 Hold the loops

Make sure the loops don't lose their height by keeping the tip of your finger on top of them as you work your next steps.

04 Continue the stitch

Ensuring that you have kept the tension loose, yarn over and insert your hook into the same stitch, yarn over and pull up another loop to the same height. You will have five loops on your hook.

05 Create another loop

Repeat — yarn over, insert hook, yarn over and draw up a loop to the same height — until you have seven unworked loops on your hook.

06 Complete the stitch

Yarn over and carefully draw the yarn through all seven loops on the hook, finishing your cluster.

TOP TIP

When completing the last step, hold gently onto the base of the worked stitches to support the structure as you draw the yarn through the stitches. The more you practise, the easier you will find it to pull through all the stitches with ease.

Popcorn stitches

Add texture to your crochet with the appropriately named popcorn stitch

Popcorn stitches are a great way to add texture to your projects and are one of the only stitches you will use where you need to remove your hook from the working loop in order to complete it. The first time you do this it is quite scary but don't panic, it will produce a fun stitch in the end and it's really easy to do. A popcorn stitch sees you create several treble (tr) crochets into a single stitch and then collect them together at the top with a chain stitch. This is what makes it stand out from the fabric. Worked in a thinner yarn it can add fun details, and in a chunky one it can add dramatic and eye-catching finishes.

01 Treble crochets

Work four treble crochets into the next stitch.

02 Remove your hook

Pull the yarn out a little further than usual, and remove your hook from the current stitch. Be careful not to let it unravel.

03 Insert your hook

Insert your hook from front to back under both loops of the top of the first treble crochet you made at the start of the popcorn stitch.

04 Get the working loop

Instead of pulling your working yarn over your hook as you would usually, insert the hook into the working loop and pull on the working yarn until it is the usual size around the hook.

05 Draw it through

Draw the working loop through the top of the first stitch and this will complete the popcorn stitch. Some patterns will dictate that you close the popcorn stitch with a chain stitch. Check the pattern that you are using. If it doesn't mention it, just finish it here.

Popcorn squares

Use the popcorn stitch to create a smart square pattern, ideal for blankets and coasters.

Popcorn - make 4 treble crochets in the specified stitch, then remove your hook from the working loop. Insert it from front to back in the top of the 1st treble crochet, then reinsert it into the working loop and draw through both loops on the hook.

01 Foundation
Chain a multiple of 4.

02 Row 1
Work 1 double crochet into the 2nd chain from your hook. *Chain 1, skip the next chain, then work a double crochet into the next one; repeat from * to the end of the row.

03 Row 2
Chain 3 (this counts as a treble crochet) and turn, then work 1 treble crochet into the next ch-1 space. *Chain 1, work a popcorn into the next ch space, chain 1, then work 1 treble crochet in the next ch space; repeat from * to the end, finishing with another treble crochet in the last double crochet stitch.

04 Row 3

Chain 1, turn, work 1 double crochet into the first stitch then chain 1. *Work 1 double crochet into the next ch space, then chain 1; repeat from * across the row, working your final double crochet into the top of the turning chain.

05 Keep on popping

Repeat Steps 03-04 to make the pattern.

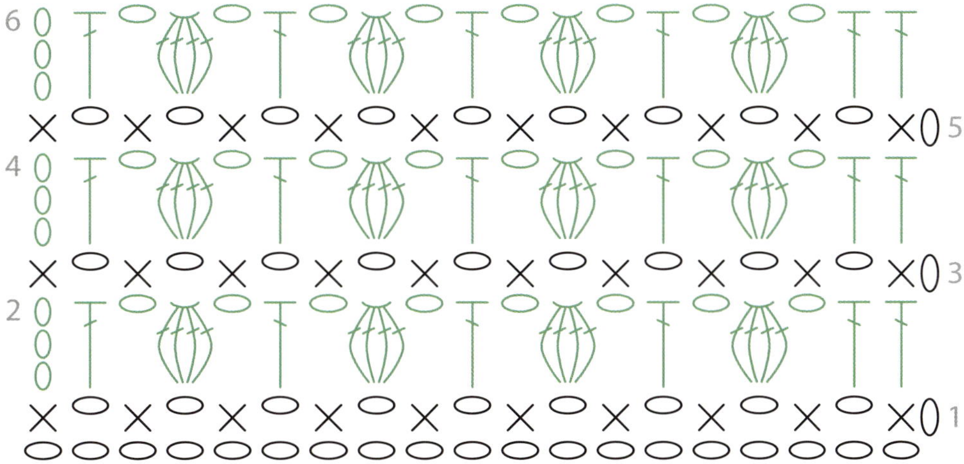

Post stitch rib

It's super easy to create a post stitch rib — all you're doing is alternating your treble crochets from front to back post to create a beautiful fabric. This is perfect for all sorts of projects from blankets and scarves to trivets and washcloths.

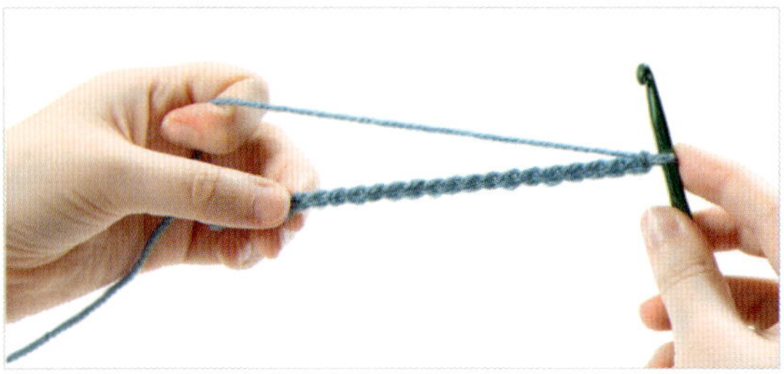

01 Foundation
Chain an even number.

02 Row 1
Work 1 treble crochet into the 4th chain from your hook, then work 1 treble crochet into each chain across.

03 Row 2
Chain 3 (this counts as a treble crochet) and turn. Work 1 treble crochet in the front post of the next stitch, then 1 treble crochet in the back post of the next one; repeat this across the row to the last stitch, work 1 treble crochet into the top of this stitch.

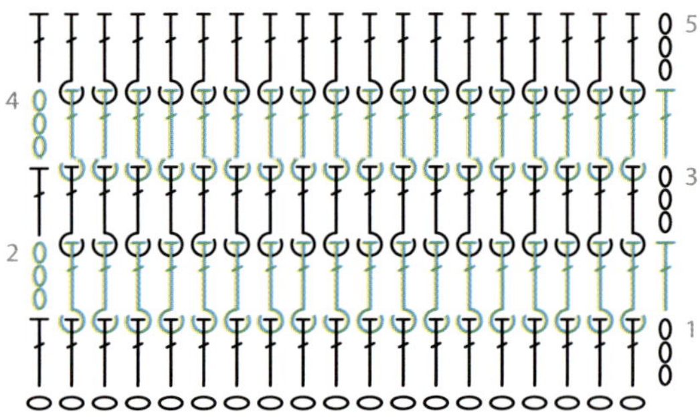

04 Keep going
Chain an even number.

Braided cable stitch

Cables are often used in knitting, but did you know that you can create them in crochet, too? Using crossed stitches and utilising posts, you can make your crochet look like it's been knitted and add some wonderful texture to your work.

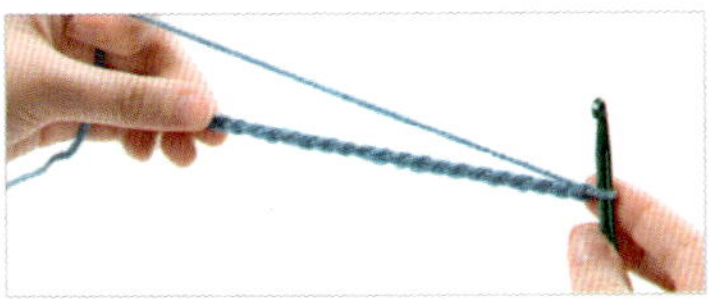

01 Foundation

Chain a multiple of 20.

02 Row 1

Work a double crochet into the 2nd chain from your hook, then double crochet to the end of the row

03 Row 2

Chain 3 and turn your work, and work 1 treble crochet into each stitch to the end of the row.

04 Row 3

Chain 1, turn, then work 1 double crochet into every stitch across, working last stitch into top of turning chain.

05 Row 4

Chain 3 and turn (counts as first treble crochet), then work 1 treble crochet into each of the next 2 double crochet stitches. *Work 1 double treble crochet into the front post of the next treble stitch on the row of treble crochets beneath, skip 1 stitch, then work 1 double treble crochet into the front post of each of the next 2 stitches on the treble crochet row before going back to work a double treble crochet in the front post of the treble that you skipped. Work 1 double treble crochet into the front post of the next treble stitch from the row beneath, then work 1 treble crochet into each of the next 3 double crochet stitches. Repeat from * to the end of the row.

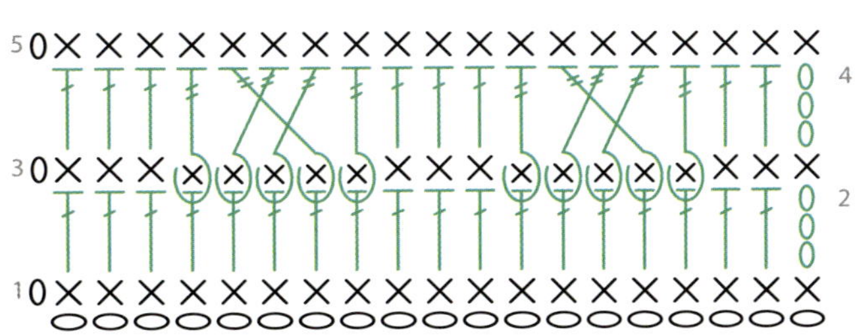

06 Row 5

Chain 1, turn your work 1 double crochet into every stitch across, working last stitch into top of turning chain.

07 Row 5

Repeat Steps 05-06 to continue the pattern.

Catherine wheel

Considered a classic, this stitch can provide somewhat of a learning curve, but the end result is definitely worth it. Once you master it you'll be able to create blankets and more that will certainly go down a treat.

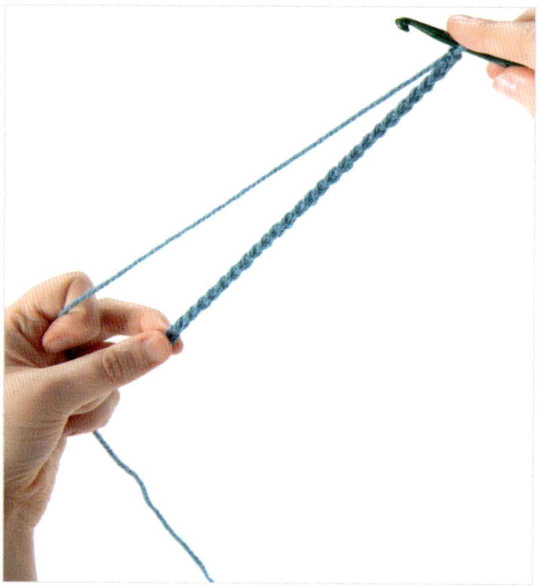

01 Foundation

Chain a multiple of 10, then an extra 7.

02 Row 1

Work 1 double crochet into the 2nd chain from your hook, and 1 double crochet into the next chain. *Skip the next 3 chains, then work 7 treble crochets into the next one, skip 3 chains, then place 1 double crochet in each of the next 3 chains; repeat from * until there are 4 chains left. Skip 3 of them, then work 4 treble crochets into the last one.

03 Row 2

We've changed colour for this row. Turn your work and chain 1, then work 1 double crochet into each of the first 2 stitches. *Chain 3, then work 7 treble crochets together across the next 7 stitches (see boxout for instructions), chain 3, then work 1 double crochet into each of the next 3 stitches; repeat from * until you have 4 stitches left. Here, chain 3, then treble crochet 4 together across the last 4 stitches.

04 Row 3

Turn your work and chain 3, then work 3 treble crochets into the first stitch. *Skip the next 3 stitches, then work 1 double crochet into each of the next 3 stitches, skip 3 stitches, then place 7 treble crochets in the loop that closed the 7 treble crochet decrease on the previous row; repeat from * until 3 chains and 2 double crochets remain unworked, then finish by skipping 3 chains and working 1 double crochet into each of the double crochets.

Treble crochet 7 together

Yarn over, insert your hook, yarn over and pull through. Then yarn over and pull through 2 loops on your hook. Yarn over again and insert your hook into the next stitch, yarn over and pull through, then yarn over and pull through 2 loops; repeat this last bit 5 more times. When you've got 8 loops on your hook, yarn over and pull through them all.

05 Row 4

We've gone back to the original colour. Turn your work and chain 3, then treble crochet 3 together across the next 3 stitches. *Chain 3, work 1 double crochet into each of the next 3 stitches, chain 3, then treble crochet 7 together across the next 7 stitches; repeat from * until you have 2 unworked stitches left. Chain 3, then work 1 double crochet into each of the remaining stitches.

06 Row 5

Turn your work and chain 1, then work 1 double crochet into the next 2 stitches. *Skip 3 chains, work 7 treble crochets into the closed loop of the 7 treble crochet decrease, skip 3 chains, then work 1 double crochet into the next 3 stitches; repeat from * until 3 chains and the turning chain remain, skip the last 3 chains and work 4 treble crochets into the top of the turning chain.

07 Build it up

Repeat Steps 03-06 to create the pattern.

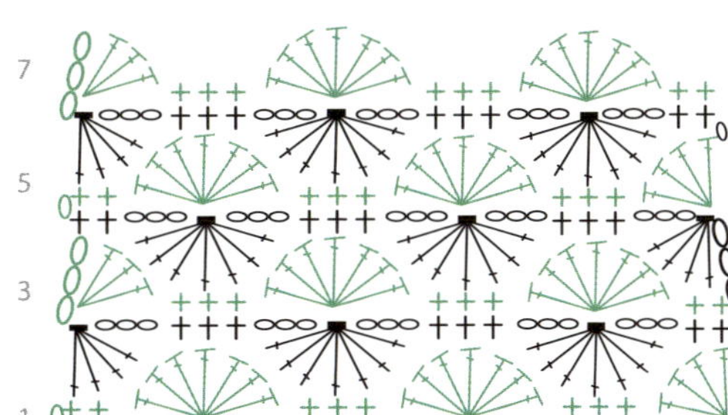

Harlequin

Perfect for intermediate crocheters, you can make some great home decor ideas like blankets and hot pads. There's a fair amount of counting involved and a lot of stitch skipping, but once you've got this stitch under your belt, you'll be glad you put the effort in.

01 Foundation

Chain a multiple of 8, plus an extra 1.

02 Row 1

In the 5th chain from your hook, work 3 treble crochets, 1 chain and 3 more treble crochets. Skip 3 chains, then work 1 double crochet into the next one. Skip 3 chains, work 3 treble crochets, 1 chain and 3 more treble crochets into the next chain, skip 3 chains, then work 1 double crochet into the next chain; repeat this sentence to the end of the row.

03 Row 2

Chain 3 and turn your work. Skip the first stitch, then treble crochet the next 3 stitches together. Chain 7, skip 1, then treble crochet the next 6 stitches together; repeat this, then treble crochet 3 together over the next 3 stitches before working 1 treble crochet into the top of the turning chain.

04 Row 3

Chain 3 and turn, then work 3 treble crochets into the first space from the row below. Work 1 double crochet around the ch-1 space of the row below (enclosing the 7 chains), then work 3 treble crochets, 1 chain and 3 more treble crochets into the centre space of the 3 stitches double crocheted together; repeat this ending with 3 treble crochets in the top of the last decrease on the previous row, then work 1 treble crochet into the top of the turning chain.

06 Row 5

Chain 1 and turn your work, then skip the first stitch and the 3 chains. Work 3 treble crochets, 1 chain and 3 more treble crochets into the centre of the 6-stitch decrease from the previous row, then work 1 double crochet into the ch-1 space of the previous row; repeat, then finish with 1 double crochet in the first of the 4 turning chains.

05 Row 4

Chain 4 and turn, then skip the first stitch. Treble crochet 6 together over the next 6 stitches, chain 7, skip 1 chain and repeat. Finish the row with 3 chains, then work 1 double crochet into the top of the turning chain.

07 Keep it up

Repeat Steps 03-06 to build more rows. If you'd like alternating colours, switch every other row.

Petal stitch

It's pretty complex, but if you've got a handle on clusters, chain spaces and counting your chains, you'll be absolutely fine with petal stitch.

01 Foundation

Chain a multiple of 11, plus an extra 3.

02 Row 1

Work 1 double crochet into the 2nd chain from your hook, chain 1, skip 1, then work 1 double crochet into the next chain. *Chain 3, skip the next 3 chains, then work 1 double crochet into the next one. Chain 3, skip 3, then work 1 double crochet into the next one. Chain 2, skip 2, then work 1 double crochet into the next chain. Repeat from * until you have 10 unworked chains left. Then, chain 3, skip 3 and work 1 double crochet into the next chain twice, chain 1, skip 1 then work 1 double crochet into the last chain.

03 Row 2

Chain 3 and turn, then work 1 tc2tog, 2 chains and another tc2tog in the same stitch. Skip the double crochet and 3 chains from the previous row and work 1 double crochet into the next double crochet. *Chain 1, skip the next 3 chains and double crochet, then work 1 tc2tog in the ch-2 space. In the same space work 2 chains and a tc2tog 3 times, then chain 1, skip the next 3 chains, and work 1 double crochet into the next double crochet. Repeat from * until you have 7 spaces left. Here, chain 1, skip 3 chains, then work a tc2tog, 2 chains and another tc2tog into the last ch-1 space. Work 1 treble crochet into the last double.

04 Row 3

Chain 1 and turn, then work 1 double crochet into the first treble. *Chain 3, then work 1 tc2tog in each of the next 4 tc2tog, chain 3, then work 1 double crochet into the next ch-2 space. Repeat from * to the end, with the last double crochet in the top of the turning chain.

05 Row 4

Chain 1 and turn, then work 1 double crochet into the first double crochet. *Chain 3, work 1 double crochet into the top of the next tc2tog, then chain 2, skip 2 and work 1 double crochet into the top of the next tc2tog. Chain 3, then work 1 double crochet into the next double. Repeat from * to end.

06 Row 5

Chain 1 and turn, then work 1 double crochet into the first double. *Chain 1, skip the next then chains, then work 1 tc2tog into the next ch-2 space. In the same space, work 2 chains and 1 tc2tog 3 times, then chain 1, skip 3 chains and work 1 double crochet into the next double. Repeat from * to the end of the row.

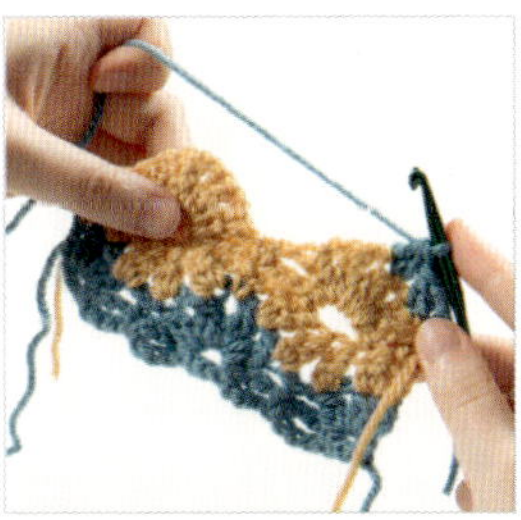

07 Row 6

Chain 3 and turn, then work 1 tc2tog into each of the next 2 tc2tog. Chain 3, work 1 double crochet in the next ch-2 space, then chain 3 again. *Work 1 tc2tog into the next 4 tc2tog, chain 3, work 1 double crochet in the next ch-2 space, then chain 3. Repeat from * until you have 2 unworked tc2tog left; here, work 1 tc2tog into each, and work 1 treble crochet into the last stitch.

08 Row 7

Chain 1 and turn, then work 1 double crochet into the first treble. Chain 1, skip 1 tc2tog, then work 1 double crochet into the next one. Chain 3, work 1 double crochet into the next double, then chain 3 again. *Work 1 double crochet into the next tc2tog, chain 3, then skip 2 tc2tog. Work 1 double crochet into the top of the next one, chain 3, work 1 double crochet into the next double, and chain 3. Repeat from * to the last 2 tc2tog; work 1 double crochet into the first, chain 1, skip the next one, then work 1 double crochet into the top of the turning chain.

09 Let it bloom

Repeat Steps 03-08 to create the pattern.

Daisy stitch

It's time to get starry-eyed with a stunning stitch. It may seem daunting at first, but once you get into the rhythm of it, you'll never want to stop. Also known as the Star stitch or Marguerite stitch.

01 Foundation
Chain an odd number.

02 Make a cluster
Insert your hook into the 2nd chain from the hook; yarn over and pull a loop through. Insert your hook into the chain next, yarn over and pull through. Continue to do this into the following three chains until there are 6 loops on your hook — yarn over and pull through all of them.

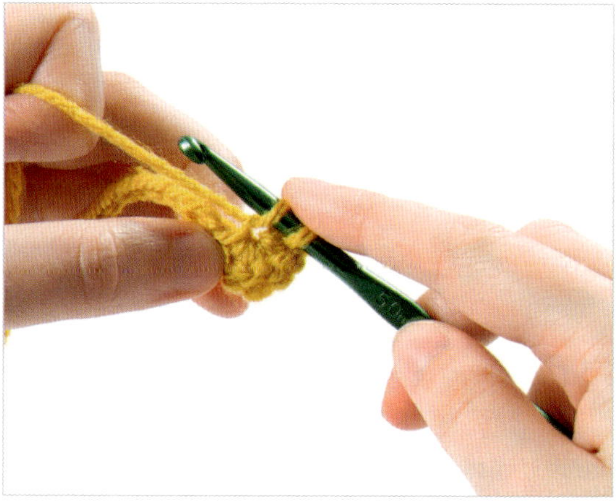

03 Chain
Make a chain, then put your hook through the hole, or eye, that this creates. Yarn over and pull through so there are two loops on your hook.

04 Another cluster

Insert your hook into the spaces between the last 2 stitches of the cluster below where you're working — yarn over and pull through so there are 3 loops on your hook. Do the same through the last chain worked for the cluster and each of the following 2 chains; there should be 6 loops on your hook. Yarn over and pull through all 6 loops on your hook.

05 Finish the row

Repeats Steps 03-04 across the row, until 1 chain remains, work a half treble crochet in the last chain.

06 Row 2

Chain 2 (this counts as the first stitch of the row) and turn. Work 2 half treble crochets into each 'eye' across the row below, then work 1 half treble crochet into the top of the turning chain.

07 Row 3

Chain 3 and turn your work. Insert your hook into the 2nd chain from the hook; yarn over and pull a loop through. Insert your hook into the chain next, yarn over and pull through. Then do the same with the following 3 stitches across the row until there are 6 loops on your hook. Yarn over and pull through. Repeat Steps 03-04, but working into stiches rather than foundation chains for Step 04.

08 Build it up

Repeat Steps 06 and 07 to continue the pattern.

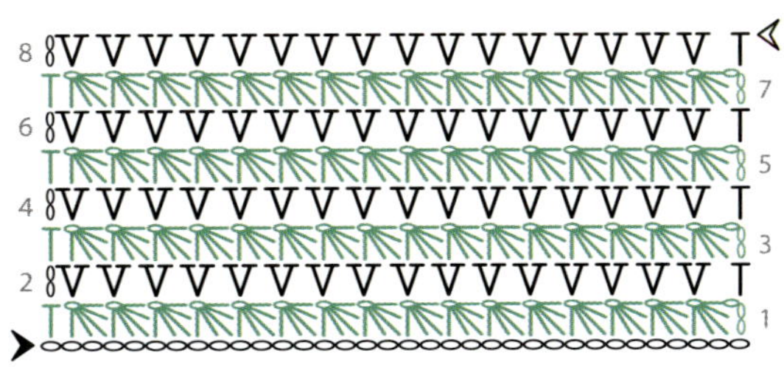

Primrose stitch

Perfect for almost everything, this stitch works up easily with just two repeated rows.

01 Foundation

Chain a multiple of 3, plus an extra 2.

02 Row 1

Work 1 double crochet into the 3rd chain from your hook, then chain 2 and work another double crochet into the same space. *Skip 2 chains, then work 1 double crochet, 2 chains and another double crochet into the next chain; repeat from * until only 2 chains remain. Skip 1 chain and work a half treble crochet in the last chain.

03 Row 2

Chain 3 and turn. Work 3 treble crochets into each ch-2 space across the row. At the end of the row, work 1 treble crochet in the top of thc turning chain.

04 Row 3

Chain 2 and turn. *Work 1 double crochet, 2 chains and another double crochet into the 2nd treble of the next shell; repeat from * until the last shell has been worked into and finish with 1 half treble crochet in the top of the turning chain.

05 Keep going

Repeat Steps 03-04 to create the pattern.

Sedge stitch

It may be just a simple repeat, but the result is a beautiful fabric that's great for everything from scarves to blankets.

01 Foundation

Chain a multiple of 3.

02 Row 1

Work 1 half treble and 1 treble crochet into the 3rd chain from your hook. *Skip 2 chains, then work 1 double crochet, 1 half treble crochet and 1 treble crochet all into the next chain, repeat from * across the row to the last 3 chains, skip 2 chains and work 1 double crochet into the last chain.

03 Row 2

Chain 1 (this counts as a double crochet) and turn, then work 1 half treble and 1 treble crochet into the 1st stitch. Skip 2 stitches, then work 1 double, 1 half treble and 1 treble crochet all into the next double crochet; repeat from * to the last 2 stitches and the turning chain. Skip the 2 stitches, then work 1 double crochet into the turning chain.

04 Keep going

Repeat Step 03 to create the pattern.

Pebble stitch

A simple mix of puffs and double crochets, there's so much you can do with this stitch, making it an easy favourite.

Puff stitch - Yarn over, insert your hook into the specified stitch and pull up a loop, then do this twice more in the same stitch. Yarn over and pull through all loops on your hook.

01 Foundation

Chain a multiple of 3, plus an extra 4.

02 Row 1

Work 1 double crochet into the 2nd chain from your hook, and in each chain across.

03 Row 2

Chain 1 and turn your work. *Work 1 double crochet into the next stitch, then 1 puff stitch into the next one; repeat from * across the row, finishing with 1 double crochet in the last stitch.

04 Row 3
Chain 1, then work 1 double crochet into every stitch across.

TOP TIP
As you build your fabric with this stitch, you'll notice that you've got a right side and a wrong side. The right side is the one where you can see the puffs.

05 Row 4
Chain 1 and turn your work. Work 1 double crochet into each of the next 2 stitches. *Work 1 puff stitch into the next stitch, then 1 double crochet into the next one; repeat from * across the row until there are 2 stitches left. Work 1 double crochet into each of them.

06 Row 5
Chain 1, then work 1 double crochet into every stitch across the row.

07 Make more pebbles
Repeat Steps 03-06 to continue the pattern.

Alpine stitch

Bring a bit of the mountains into your makes with this gorgeous stitch. Its density brings warmth even in the bitterest winters, and it's perfect for cardigans, jumpers and more. This Stitch is also known as the Alternating treble crochet or Front post stitch.

01 Foundation
Chain an odd number.

02 Row 1
Work a treble crochet in the 3rd chain from your hook, and then in each chain across.

03 Row 2
Chain 1 and turn. Then make 1 double crochet in each stitch across.

04 Row 3

Chain 2 and turn. Work 1 treble crochet in the 1st stitch. *Work 1 treble crochet around the front post of the treble below the next stitch, then work 1 treble in the next stitch; repeat from * until the end of the row, finishing with a treble crochet in the last stitch.

05 Row 4

Chain 1 and turn. Work a double crochet in every stitch across the row.

06 Row 5

Chain 2 and turn. Work 1 treble crochet into each of the first two stitches. *Work 1 treble crochet around the front post of the treble below the next stitch, then work 1 treble crochet in the next stitch; repeat from * until the last stitch finishing with a treble crochet in this stitch.

07 Keep building

Repeat Steps 03-06 to create the pattern.

Waffle stitch

Ever wanted to re-create breakfast food with crochet? Use posts to work up this unique pattern.

01 Foundation

Chain a multiple of 3, plus 2 extra.

02 Row 1

Work a treble crochet into the 4th chain from your hook, then work a treble crochet in every chain across.

03 Row 2

Chain 3 (this counts as a treble crochet) and turn. *Work 1 treble crochet in the front post of the next stitch, then 1 treble crochet in each of the next 2 stitches; repeat from * to the last 2 stitches.

Here, work 1 treble crochet in the front post of the next stitch, then 1 treble crochet in the top of the turning chain.

04 Row 3

Chain 3 and turn your work. *Work 1 treble crochet into the next stitch, then 1 treble crochet into the front post of each of the next 2 stitches; repeat from * to the last 2 stitches. Here, work 1 treble crochet into the next stitch, and then 1 treble crochet into the top of the turning chain.

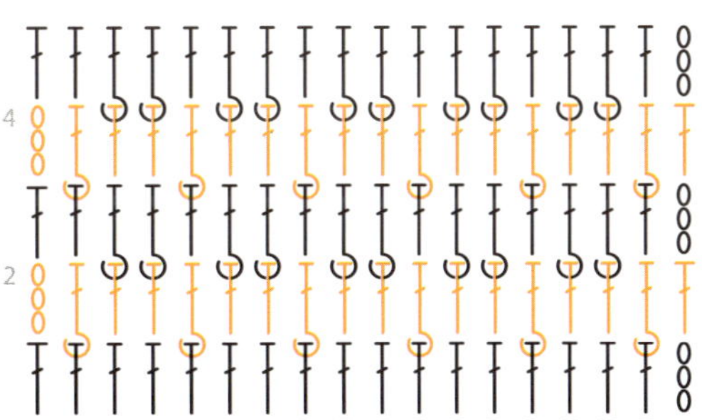

05 Make your waffle

Repeat Steps 03-04 to continue the pattern.

Basketweave

Posts can be used to make some beautiful stitches, like basketweave. Once you get the hang of it, it's pretty easy, so why not have a go?

01 Foundation

Chain a multiple of 6, plus an extra 4.

02 Row 1

Work 1 treble crochet into the 4th chain from your hook, and in every chain across.

03 Row 2

Chain 3 and turn. Work 1 treble crochet in the front post of the next 3 stitches, then 1 treble crochet in the back post of the next 3 stitches; repeat this across to the last stitch. Here, work 1 treble crochet into the top of the turning chain.

04 Row 3

Repeat Step 03.

05 Row 4

Chain 3 and turn. Work 1 treble crochet into the back post of the next 3 stitches, then 1 treble crochet in the front post of the next 3 stitches; repeat this across to the last stitch. Here, work 1 treble crochet into the top of the turning chain. Repeat this step.

TOP TIP

This stitch is great for blankets when it's worked in a thicker yarn.

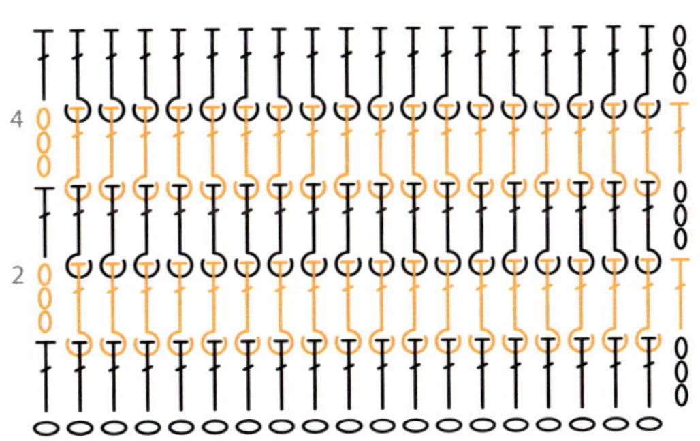

06 Building the basket

Repeat Steps 03-05 to create the pattern.

Triangle spaces

Creating this open weave is much easier than you think so long as you remember to count!

01 Foundation

Chain a multiple of 6, plus an extra 2.

02 Row 1

Work 1 double crochet into the 2nd chain from your hook. Work 1 double crochet in the next chain, chain 3, skip 3, then work 1 double crochet into the next chain. *Chain 1, skip the next chain, then work 1 double crochet into the next one. Chain 3, skip 3, then work 1 double crochet in the next chain. Repeat from * across to the end, then finish with 1 double crochet in the last chain.

03 Row 2

Chain 1, turn and work 1 double crochet into the next stitch. Chain 2, then work 3 treble crochets into the next ch-3 space. *Chain 2, work 1 double crochet into the next ch-1 space, chain 2, then work 3 treble crochets into the next ch-3 space. Repeat from * across until you have 2 unworked stitches left. Here, chain 2, skip the next stitch, then work 1 double crochet into the last one.

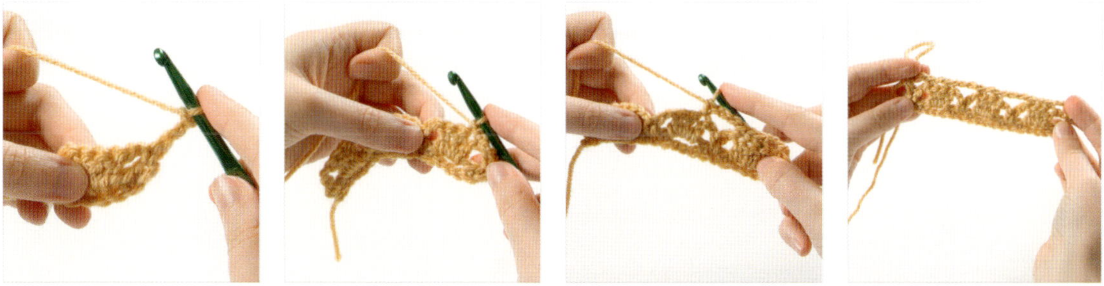

04 Row 3

Chain 4 (this counts as a treble and a chain) and turn your work. Place 1 double crochet in the next treble, chain 1, skip the next stitch, then place 1 double crochet in the next one. *Chain 3, work 1 double crochet into the next treble crochet, chain 1, skip the next treble, then double crochet in the next one. Repeat from * to the end of the row, finishing by chaining 1 and working 1 treble crochet in the last double.

05 Row 4

Chain 3 (this counts as a treble crochet), turn your work and place 1 treble crochet in the next ch-1 space. Chain 2, then work 1 double crochet into the next ch-1 space. *Chain 2, work 3 treble crochets into the next ch-3 space, chain 2, then work 1 double crochet in the next ch-1 space. Repeat from * across to the last space. Here, chain 2, then work 2 treble crochets into the turning chain space.

06 Row 5

Chain 1, turn, then work 1 double crochet in each of the next 2 stitches. Chain 3, *work 1 double crochet into the next treble, chain 1, skip the next treble, then work 1 double crochet into the next one and chain 3. Repeat from * across until you have 2 unworked stitches remaining in the row. Work 1 double crochet into the next treble crochet, and then another in the top of the turning chain.

07 Keep going

Repeat Steps 03-06 to create the pattern.

Tumbling blocks

Bring a little playfulness into your crochet with this fun stitch.

01 Foundation

Chain a multiple of 8, plus an extra 5.

TOP TIP

Take your time when working up your first practice swatch of this stitch — some care needs to be taken to make sure that you're putting your stitches in the right places.

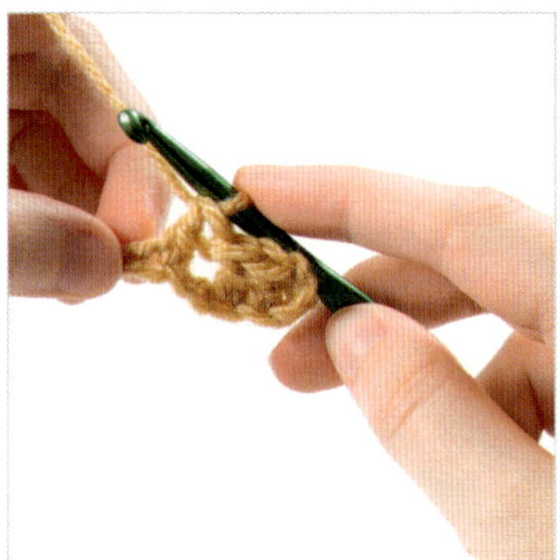

02 Row 1

Work 1 treble crochet into the 4th chain from your hook. *Work 1 treble crochet into the next chain, skip 2, then work 1 treble crochet into the next chain. Chain 3, then work 3 treble crochets around the post of the treble you just made, skip 2 chains and then work 1 treble crochet in each of the next 2 chains. Repeat from * to 1 chain from the end, work 1 treble crochet into this chain.

03 Row 2

Chain 3 (this counts as a treble crochet) and turn. Work 1 treble crochet into each of the next 2 stitches, *chain 2, work 1 double crochet in the ch-3 space, chain 2, skip next treble crochet, then work 1 treble crochet into each of the next 3 trebles on the previous row; repeat from * to end, working the last treble into the top of the turning chain.

04 Row 3

Chain 3 and turn. *Work 1 treble crochet into the next 2 stitches, skip 2 chain, work 1 treble crochet into the double crochet on the previous row, chain 3, work 3 treble crochets around the post of the treble you just made, skip 2 chain, work 1 treble crochet in the next treble on the previous row. Repeat from * until the last stitch and turning chain. Here, work 1 treble crochet into the next stitch, then another in the top of the turning chain.

05 Keep tumbling

Repeat Steps 03-04 to create the pattern.

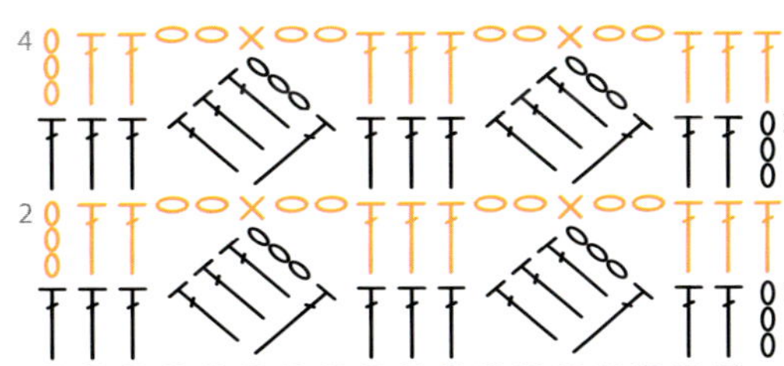

Edges & Finishes

Complete your work with a creative flourish, from fringes to flower motifs.

"In crochet, a motif is any sort of smaller piece of crochet you create that's intended to be part of a bigger project"

Basic edging

When you've finished working a flat piece, a simple border made of double crochets will help straighten the sides and give a neat finish

You may find that the edges of a flat piece of crochet worked in rows can tend to become very wavy or unattractively distorted. This happens to all crocheters at some point, and it is most likely caused by fluctuating tension. But not to worry, there's a simple solution that will give you crisp, neat edges every single time — adding a border of double crochets. This adds a degree of uniformity to all four edges, as without a border the side edges look very different to the top and bottom edges. If you simply want to neaten up your piece and create a seamless looking edge, add your border in the same colour as the rest of the work. However, a border in a contrasting colour will stand out and can add a touch of character to your work.

If your piece has a distinct front and back, make sure you add the border with the front of the piece facing you.

Function over style

Make the slip stitch (sl st)

02 Double crochet

Make a double crochet into the same stitch.

01 Join the yarn

Insert your hook into the stitch at the top right corner of the work. Draw up a loop of the yarn you will be using for the edging, making sure to keep it tight. Chain one.

03 Along the top

Make a double crochet into every stitch along the top of your work, except the last stitch of the row.

04 Make a corner

Into the last stitch of the row, make three double crochets (dc). This will keep the corner square and help it lie flat.

05 Rotate it

You will now work along the left-hand side of the piece, so rotate the work so you can work into the stitches. Insert your hook into the edge stitch (making sure it only goes under one or two loops) instead of around the entire stitch.

06 Make another corner

Work along the edge until you get to the corner. Work three double crochets into the corner stitch. Rotate the work to continue along the bottom, making one stitch in each stitch of the foundation chain.

07 Work on the next side

When you reach the end of the foundation chain, again make three double crochets in the corner stitch. Rotate and work along the side in the same way as you did for the first side.

TOP TIP

If you want to create a more decorative edge around your piece, make a double crochet border first, as this provides a stable foundation to work more stitches into.

08 Slip stitch

When you reach the last corner, make three double crochets and then join with a slip stitch (sl st) to the first stitch of the border. Fasten off. Your edging is complete.

Reverse double crochet

Create a non-stretchy cord edge with the reverse double crochet

Also known as a crab stitch, the reverse double crochet (rdc) is worked in the opposite direction to what you are used to. Admittedly, it can take a little while to get the hang of this, as it completely goes against the natural order of all things crochet. You will start at the left-hand side of the piece and work towards the right. This means that each of the stitches will be twisted so that the usual V formation is hidden and the edge is neatly finished. Note that you can't crochet into a reverse double crochet as it doesn't offer a solid entry point, so make sure you only ever use this technique as a pretty edging to the end of your project.

"Each of the stitches will be twisted so that the usual V formation is hidden and the edge is neatly finished"

TOP TIP

If you work too quickly your yarn could snag around the last stitch you made and the stitches could tangle together. If this happens, just undo the stitch and start again. Take your time!

Reverse double crochet

Create an elegant bobbled edging

01 Fasten on

Choose any point along the edge of your piece of fabric and chain one. You will work into the previous stitch, the one to the right of your hook, not the one to your left!

02 Start the stitch

Insert your hook as your would usually from front to back.

Work into the same stitch

If you're working all the way around, work your final reverse double crochet into the same stitch as where you fastened on, as this will currently be unworked.

03 Hook facing forward

Yarn over (yo) and draw up a loop, making sure your hook faces towards the left as it would usually. If you twist your hook, you will end up with a mirrored version of a standard double crochet (dc), not a reverse stitch.

04 Complete the stitch

Now complete the stitch as you would a normal double crochet, yarn over and draw through both loops on the hook.

05 Keep going

Continue to work backwards along your edge, making sure not to twist your hook!

06 Reverse around the corner

If you are going around a 90-degree corner, work three reverse double crochets into the same stitch.

Fringe

Create a fringe to embellish your scarves or other projects

Adding a fringe at the end of any project can be the final detail you need to make it complete, especially when it comes to scarves. You can customise it in several ways, depending on the colour and the length of the fringe, the number of strands per section that you tie on, and you can also vary the gaps between each knot. If you're using the same colour as your project for your fringe, you can incorporate the ends instead of having to weave them in. And if you're using contrasting colours then you can use it to help secure your weaved-in ends!

It should be easy to figure out how many strands you need for most projects, by counting how many stitches you want to weave your fringe into, knowing how many strands you wish to put into each stitch, and multiplying them together. If you want to avoid doing any maths, you can simply cut some at a time, tie them on and keep going until you're all done!

Fringe technique

Add some detail to your project

01 Round one

Cut a piece of card to the size you require. Make sure that it creates lengths roughly 2cm (1in) longer than the desired fringe length to account for the knots in the yarn.

02 Cut the yarn

Take a sharp pair of scissors to the edge of the card, slip a blade behind the yarn and cut. Each strand will now be the same length!

03 Count up the strands

Decide on how many strands you want on each part of your fringe, remembering that one strand of yarn will create two in the piece of fringe. Fold the strands in half.

04 Pull it through

Using your crochet hook, insert the head through the stitch you wish to add the fringe to. Insert the hook into the middle of the strands.

05 Pull through

Carefully draw the strands through, leaving a loop big enough to slip your fingers into. Alternatively, you can use your hook to pull through the strands.

06 Secure the ends

Once you have pulled all the strands through the loop, be careful not to accidentally pull on one strand more than the others, as this will make the fringe wonky. Pull until the knot is nice and tight. Now repeat until you're finished.

Picot edging

Give your work a delicate finish with a picot edging, often used on clothing and lace pieces

Quite simply, picot edging is a collection of chain stitches that can be added to the edge of your crochet project. They are brought together by a double crochet (dc) into the next stitch (or into the bottom of the chain) or by skipping stitches to create larger loops, also know as open picot. It has the benefit of being really simple to do while managing to look incredibly effective. You can make your picot stitches as long or as short as you like, from using only two extra chains to create a small bobble or a whole load of them to create a fun fringe effect.

If you are following a pattern it should state what type of picot edging, and whether to go into the bottom of the chain or into the next stitch (or, of course, how many stitches to skip!).

"You can make your picot stitches as long or as short as you like, from using only two extra chains to create a small bobble or a whole load of them to create a fun fringe effect"

Picot edging

Add a border to your garments

01 Fasten on

Fasten on your yarn to any stitch, chain one. Double crochet into the first stitch and then chain three.

02 Into the loop

Work into the front loop and left vertical bar of the stitch at the base of your chain.

03 Slip stitch

Complete your picot stitch with a slip stitch (sl st). Insert your hook into the vertical bar of the double crochet below, draw up a loop and draw it through the loop on the hook.

04 Double crochet

Now do a few double crochets along the edge in order to space out the picot edge.

TOP TIP

It is best to count your stitches before you start and do a little bit of maths to figure out how many picot stitches you want, and how often they will need to occur.

05 Picot again

Now repeat Steps 01 to 03 to create another picot. And repeat.

06 Around the bend

To picot on a corner, continue as your would for a normal double crocheted edge, making three double crochets into the corner stitch. Continue to count your stitches and make sure you keep the gaps between them the same.

Flower motifs

Add embellishments to your projects by creating and attaching separate flowers

Crochet flowers are quick and easy to make. They only take a couple of rounds and a few different stitches to create something that looks more complicated than it actually is. Added to a child's cardigan or to a crocheted hat, these details can really bring a project together. You don't just have to use them as embellishments, however, you could attach a safety pin to the wrong side of the finished flower to use it as a brooch all on its own. Here we have used just one colour but you could easily use multiple hues to give your flowers a boost. You can make flowers with any size yarn, just make sure you have the correct size hook to suit.

Simple flower

Make an easy flower in two rounds

01 Magic ring

Make a magic ring and then chain one.

02 Round one

Double crochet (dc) into your magic ring and then chain two. Repeat this five more times so you end up with six. Pull the ring closed and join it to the first stitch with a slip stitch (sl st).

03 Second round

Into each chain space do the following: slip stitch, chain two, two treble crochets (tr), chain two, slip stitch. Repeat this six times, and your petals will be complete. Fasten off and weave in the ends.

Double flower

Try a more detailed design

01 Start the flower

This flower is worked in a continuous spiral, so don't join the rounds at the end. Start with a magic ring — so six double crochets into it, and then pulling it closed.

02 Round two

Into each stitch from round one do the following: chain two, treble crochet in front loop, chain two, slip stitch in front loop of same stitch.

03 Round three

Fold the petals forwards to expose the back loops. For round three you will work into the back loops of round one. In each of the back loops work the following: chain one, treble crochet. Then slip stitch into the first chain space (ch-sp). You will have made six treble crochets.

04 Final round

Chain two, two treble crochets in the same chain space at the bottom of the chain you just created. Chain two, slip stitch in same chain space. *Chain two, two treble crochets in next chain space, chain two, slip stitch in same chain space. Repeat from * five times. Make six petals. Fasten off and weave in ends.

Abbreviations

UK stitch name	Abbreviation	Symbol	Description
back loop	**BL**		The loop furthest from you at the top of the stitch.
back post double crochet	**BPdc**		Yarn over, insert the hook from the back to the front, then to the back around the post of the next stitch, yarn over and draw up a loop, (yarn over and draw through two loops) twice.
chain(s)	**ch(s)**		Yarn over and draw through the loop on the hook.
chain space(s)	**ch-sp(s)**		The space beneath one or more chains.
double crochet	**dc**	× or +	Insert the hook into the next stitch and draw up a loop, yarn over and draw through both loops on the hook.
double crochet 2 together	**dc2tog**	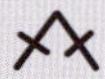	(Insert the hook into the next stitch and draw up a loop) twice, yarn over and draw through all three loops on the hook.
double treble crochet	**dtr**		Yarn over twice, insert the hook into the next stitch and draw up a loop, (yarn over and draw through two loops on the hook) three times.
front loop	**FL**		The loop closest to you at the top of the stitch.
front post treble crochet	**FPtr**		Yarn over, insert the hook from the front to the back to the front around the post of the next stitch, yarn over and draw up a loop, (yarn over and draw through two loops) twice.
half treble crochet	**htr**		Yarn over, insert the hook into the next stitch and draw up a loop, yarn over and draw through all three loops on the hook.
repeat	**rep**		Replicate a series of given instructions.
skip	**sk**		Pass over a stitch or stitches — do not work into it.
slip stitch	**sl st or ss**	⬬ or ●	Insert the hook into the next stitch, draw up a loop through the stitch and the loop on the hook.
stitch(es)	**st(s)**		A group of one or more loops of yarn pulled through each other in a specified order until only 1 remains on the crochet hook.
treble crochet	**tr**		Yarn over, insert the hook into the next stitch and draw up a loop, (yarn over and draw through two loops on the hook) twice.
treble crochet 2 together	**tr2tog**		(Yarn over, insert the hook into the next stitch and draw up a loop, yarn over and draw through two loops on the hook) twice, yarn over and draw through all three loops on the hook.
turning chain	**t-ch**		The chain made at the start of a row to bring your hook and yarn up to the height of the next row.
yarn over	**yo**		Pass the yarn over the hook so the yarn is caught in the throat of the hook.